FROM THE OTHER SHORE

and

THE RUSSIAN PEOPLE AND SOCIALISM

Also by Alexander Herzen

CHILDHOOD, YOUTH AND EXILE
(Parts I and II of *My Past and Thoughts*)
translated by J. D. Duff
with an introduction by Isaiah Berlin
The World's Classics
(forthcoming)

Alexander Herzen

FROM THE OTHER SHORE

Translated from the Russian by
MOURA BUDBERG

and

THE RUSSIAN PEOPLE AND SOCIALISM

Translated from the French by
RICHARD WOLLHEIM

With an introduction by
ISAIAH BERLIN

Oxford New York Toronto Melbourne
OXFORD UNIVERSITY PRESS
1979

Oxford University Press, Walton Street, Oxford OX2 6DP

OXFORD LONDON GLASGOW

NEW YORK TORONTO MELBOURNE WELLINGTON

KUALA LUMPUR SINGAPORE JAKARTA HONG KONG TOKYO

DELHI BOMBAY CALCUTTA MADRAS KARACHI

NAIROBI DAR ES SALAAM CAPE TOWN

First published 1956 by George Weidenfeld and Nicolson Limited
First published as an Oxford University Press paperback with revised Introduction and Bibliographical Note 1979

British Library Cataloguing in Publication Data

Herzen, Alexander,
From the other shore.—The Russian people and socialism.—first ed. reprinted.
1. France—Politics and Government—1830–1848
France—Politics and Government—1848–1852
3. Labour and Labouring Classes—Russian—History—19th century.
I. Title II. Herzen, Alexander. The Russian people and socialism
944.07 D.C 266.5 7A–41338
ISBN 0–19–281268–8

Printed in England by
G. A. Pindar & Son Ltd., Scarborough

CONTENTS

INTRODUCTION

Isaiah Berlin

ALEXANDER IVANOVICH HERZEN was born in his father's house in Moscow on April 6th, 1812, some six months before Napoleon occupied the city; he died in Paris on January 21st, 1870, during the last days of the Second Empire. His father, Ivan Alekseyevich Yakovlev, came of an ancient, wealthy and aristocratic Moscow family. During his travels abroad he met Luisa Haag, the daughter of a minor official in Württemberg, and returned to Moscow with her. He established her as mistress of his household, but, perhaps for reasons of social disparity, did not marry her. Her son Alexander did not inherit his father's name, and was called Herzen almost as if to mark the circumstances of his birth. He seems to have been treated in every other respect as his father's true son and heir: he received the normal education of a well-born young Russian of those days, and after a succession of private tutors, among whom he remembered best a French émigré with crypto-Jacobin views, and a Russian student of mildly radical leanings, he entered Moscow University in 1829, and attended lectures on philosophy, literature and the natural sciences, or what went under that name in Moscow at that time. Like other young men in Europe in the new dawn of radical thought, he admired the writings of French socialists and German Idealist philosophers, and defended their views with fervour and wit in the Moscow literary *salons*. His contemporaries liked (or disliked) him for his gaiety and charm, his passionate and uncompromising character, his overflowing imagination and wide culture, his sensitiveness, his rapid, darting, bold and, as one of his friends called it, 'predatory' intellect, his dialectical skill, above all his singular combination of generous moral idealism and a biting, intolerant, often highly destructive, ironical humour. He found himself politically suspect comparatively early in his university career, probably for discussing and supporting left-wing social views, and his subsequent career in government service was broken by two periods of exile, in each case for entertaining 'dangerous' ideas. Both in exile and in Moscow and St Petersburg he wrote, and occasionally published, essays, short stories and novels, imbued with that spirit of violent protest against the political and social environment of his time which in varying degrees characterized all the *revoltés* young intellectuals in Russia during the reign of Nicholas I, and in particular his friends Turgenev, Bakunin, Stankevich, Granovsky, Belinsky, Ogaryov and other members of the remarkable group of young radicals who created the traditions of the Russian intelligentsia.

Herzen's early essays are typical of the preoccupations of the time: they deal with historical and philosophical topics—the 'new' French sociological school of historians (he actually translated Augustin-Thierry's *Merovingian Stories*), the nationalism of the Slavophils, distinctions in subject and method between the various arts and sciences. There are semi-Hegelian disquisitions on the true vocation of man in the nineteenth century and on the relations of nature to history; fragments of autobiography; an elegant and amusing account of the difference between the spirit of Petersburg and that of Moscow; and finally a lengthy dissertation on the rival dangers of dilettantism and pedantry. The last of these essays is perhaps the acutest and best written. Herzen draws an entertaining and very telling contrast between easily excited but superficial amateurs who view facts through a telescope and do not see the trees for the wood, as against the microscopic pedantry of professional scholars, happy victims of the worst German academic models. He enjoys himself equally at the expense of both these failures of perspective, but, on the whole, is severer towards the amateurs who are terrified by the prospect of losing their own unique individuality in preoccupation with scholarly pursuits, than to the professionals who see nothing, and cling timorously to their own narrowly specialized field.

As for Herzen's novels and stories, they are typical radical denunciations of conventional morality and social oppression, written under the influence of Schiller, the French romantics, George Sand, and the passionate 'literature of protest' of the period. His best novel, *Who is to Blame?*, deals with a situation common enough at that time—of a rich and unhappy young Russian landowner (the 'superfluous man') vainly struggling against his environment, a figure to become celebrated later in the novels of Herzen's contemporaries, Goncharov, Dostoevsky, Tolstoy, but especially Turgenev—the prototype of many a Russian Hamlet, too idealistic and too honest to accept the squalor and the lies of conventional society, too weak and too civilized to work effectively for their destruction, and consequently displaced from his proper function and doomed to poison his own life and the lives of others by neurotic behaviour induced by the vices of a society which sins against the moral ideals which the author holds dear, a society either irremediably corrupt, or still capable of regeneration, according to the author's social or religious beliefs.

On his father's death in the spring of 1846, Herzen,

now financially secure, asked himself what career he was to pursue. He was ambitious and knew this; he wished to make his mark in the world, to build himself a monument. His spectacular failure to be a model government official had shown him plainly that there was no room in Russia for a high-spirited, gifted, violently liberty loving, romantically inclined aristocratic young man who wished to enter the field of public activity. In the winter of 1847, taking with him his wife, his mother and his entire household, he left for Paris. He never saw Russia again.

After slowly crossing Germany and France the travellers reached the French capital. In Paris Herzen plunged headlong into the great ferment of ideas and emotions in which the political émigrés, gathered there from every European country, lived their agitated lives. The arresting quality of his mind and personality made an impression even in that extraordinary assembly of talent and genius; he was, with Bakunin, almost the first denizen of the barbarous and frightening Russian Empire to be recognized as an equal by the political thinkers of the fabled West—as an equal intellectually, and not, like other cultured Russian travellers, as a gifted and agreeable intellectual tourist, or an indolent and curious passer-by. A new revolution was clearly gathering in Europe and Herzen was caught in its mounting tide.

During 1848–9 he travelled in Switzerland, Savoy and Italy, and his descriptions of the stirring events which he witnessed in Rome and Paris during the *annus mirabilis* are a masterpiece of acute observation and literary talent. He does not conceal his sympathies: he detests kings and priests, soldiers and policemen, bankers, bourgeois politicians, authors of appeals to good sense and order; he idealizes the 'blue blouses'—the workers of Paris—and pays a glowing tribute to the noble and simple-hearted plebeian masses in Rome, he is for republicans, for revolutionaries, for the triumvirs of Rome, for Garibaldi, for the leader of the Roman populace whom he calls Cicerovacchio, for Saffi and Mazzini. He speaks with affection and irony about his friend Bakunin, the greatest of Russian political agitators, invaluable on the first day of a revolution, disastrous on the second; he admires and likes Proudhon, Michelet, the Swiss radical James Fazy; his most intimate friends are the revolutionary German poet, Wagner's friend, Georg Herwegh, and Herwegh's wife. By a bitter irony of circumstance the relationship between himself, his wife (and first cousin) Natalie, and Herwegh began more and more to resemble the plot of his own *Who is to Blame?*, in which a fascinating stranger falls in love with the happily married wife of a man who trusts him, and duly destroys himself and his friends. Herzen perceived this analogy himself and rejected it with indignation. His 'superfluous' hero Bel'tov was at least capable of moral agony and heroic martyrdom, whereas Herwegh now seemed to him a contemptible philistine and scoundrel, married to an equally repulsive wife. Herzen set down the details of the entire episode with a self-revealing candour and painful precision, oddly unexpected in so proud and sensitive a man. Natalie, betrayed by her lover, returned to her husband, to die in his arms a year later. Blow followed blow. Herzen's mother and one of his sons were drowned in a tempest off Genoa. The revolution in Europe collapsed ignominiously in one country after another. In a state of acute personal and political misery, Herzen left France and settled in the free but, to him, bleak and chilly atmosphere of England. He lived in and near London intermittently until the middle '60s.

In London he established his own 'free' printing press, and in the '50s began to publish two periodicals in Russian, *The Polar Star* (the first issue appeared in 1855) and *The Bell* (in 1857), which marked the birth of systematic revolutionary agitation—and conspiracy—by Russian exiles against the Tsarist régime.

Herzen's house—or houses, for he moved from one to another constantly—became a place of pilgrimage for the radical exiles of many lands, particularly Poles, with whom he was one of the few Russians to remain on warm terms all his life, and Italians, to whom he early lost his heart. His attitude to Frenchmen was more reserved: the solemnity, the rhetoric, the monomania of the *ci-devant* tribunes of the people and their entourage offered too much material for his highly developed sense of the ridiculous. He found the mystical Hungarian worship of Kossuth more bizarre than awe-inspiring; the Germans, in particular Karl Marx and his friends, he found unbearable. As for the English, he met few among them. He paid a visit to the aged and senile Owen; he corresponded with Carlyle; he respected Mill. But, on the whole, little attention was paid to him in England, and he responded with mingled admiration and dislike for his hosts. His warmest friendships remained those of his early years, with his Russian friends and contemporaries—first and foremost with the poet Ogaryov, with whom he set up house in London in the '50s, and with Bakunin, who had escaped from his Siberian exile, and whom, in the '60s, he viewed, as before, with a mixture of irritation and indulgence. He delighted in the stream of Russian visitors who came to see him—writers and journalists, liberal aristocrats with a taste for taking political risks, old Slavophil opponents, vehement young radicals who thought him a useless relic of a previous epoch, dissident Orthodox priests, university professors, old acquaintances of all sorts, whom his growing prestige drew towards what had in fact become the official centre of the opposition to the Russian government. Herzen became a European celebrity, and *The Bell*, which specialized in exposing specific abuses and in naming names, in the heyday of its fame—the late '50s and early '60s—exercised a unique influence even in official circles in St Petersburg. After the suppression of the Polish Revolution in 1863, its influence—it had supported the Poles in the face of almost universal patriotic indignation in Russia—began to fall precipitately. After lingering in a desultory manner in London, where he lived intermittently and not too happily with Ogaryov's gifted and neurasthenic wife, Herzen travelled in Italy and Switzerland, and died in Paris on January 21st, 1870. He is buried in Nice and his statue stands above his tomb.

Early in his London period he began his celebrated autobiography or biographical memoirs—the *Past and Reflections*, on which his fame as a writer ultimately rests. This work is a literary and political masterpiece, worthy to stand beside the great Russian novels of the nineteenth century. The book has no formal design but consists of a succession of episodes connected by a loose chronological sequence in the course of which Herzen records private and public experiences, draws vignettes of personalities and predicaments, offers analyses of present and future social and political conditions both in Europe and Russia, together with scattered personal observations, fragments of a diary, epigrams, historical and psychological sketches, travel notes, accounts of the impact upon him of, or of the role played by, political, historical ideas, vivid and exact descriptions of his feelings, of incidents in his life, encounters, conversations, confessions, entertaining and memorable sketches of the characteristics and eccentricities of various groups of émigrés in London and elsewhere, of episodes in their lives, and of their reactions to one another and to their English hosts—this vast and apparently heterogeneous amalgam held together by a gift for narrative and descriptive writing which, in its own kind, has never been excelled. *Past and Reflections* is an autobiography of the first order of genius, and remains pre-eminent even in the nineteenth century, which was exceedingly rich in this *genre*. It has been translated into several languages, but it is only in the author's native land that it is recognized as a major classic, comparable in quality and scope with *War and Peace*.

Besides this famous work, Herzen, during more than twenty years of uninterrupted activity as a publicist—the voice of free Russia abroad, calling for revolution—poured out a mass of articles, letters, essays, proclamations, the best of which are original masterpieces both of journalism and of art. He was one of the most perspicacious observers of the European scene in the nineteenth century—in this respect only Marx and Tocqueville are comparable to him—and the *Letters from France and Italy* (he called an earlier version *Letters from Avenue Marigny*), which he sent in instalments to his friends in Moscow, to be printed in the radical Russian journal, *The Contemporary*, contain the best general analyses of the political and social scene of the West just before and during the revolution of 1848. He continued to observe, record and analyse public and private life in France, in England, in Russia, in articles and improvisations, all his life. Unsystematic, brilliantly entertaining and permanently valuable, these fragments are scattered in the thirty volumes of the great Soviet edition of his works, and still form a unique account of the life of Europe in the middle years of the last century.

More important than most of these historical sketches is the long essay which Herzen entitled *From the Other Shore.*[1] This is an attempt to assess the consequences and point the moral of the final failure of the European revolutions of 1848. As a piece of writing this essay exhibits, at any rate in the original, that combination of acuteness, irony, imagination, moral distinction, fiery, often poetical, eloquence, and penetrating intellectual force coupled with an elegance of style and poignant feeling, which forms the peculiar quality of Herzen's personality as a writer. It is designed as a *post mortem* on the liberal and democratic doctrines—and phraseology—which had suffered shipwreck in the failure of the revolution, and contains ethical and political ideas which are of interest not simply as scattered *pensées*, but as an expression of a moral and social philosophy of considerable originality, possessing affinities with views fully articulated only in our own time.

From the Other Shore deals with the débâcle of 1848 neither in the detached and ironical mood of Tocqueville's celebrated memoir, nor as an application of a specific theory of history to contemporary events like the two essays on the same theme by Karl Marx. Herzen wrote neither to justify individuals and parties, nor to demonstrate a specific philosophy of history. But he resembled Marx and Tocqueville in that he, too, sought to describe the situation, to examine the views and ambitions and desires of the various parties and individuals and classes, and their social and historical roots; to consider the manner and the causes of the betrayal of the revolution by

[1]So far as I know, here translated for the first time into English.

its principal supporters; to expose the emptiness and the confusions of the social and political programmes themselves—and to trace this to specific fears, muddles and evasions on the part of those high-minded but craven liberals who 'at the same time undermine the old order and cling to it, light the fuse and try to stop the explosion'.

Herzen's essay is, in the main, a frontal attack upon the doctrine at that time preached by almost every left-wing orator in Europe (with the notable exception of Proudhon, Stirner and a handful of anarchists to whom no one listened), about the sacred human duty of offering up oneself—or others—upon the altar of some great moral or political cause—some absolute principle or abstract noun capable of stirring strong emotion, like Nationality, or Democracy, or Equality, or Humanity, or Progress. For Herzen these are merely modern versions of ancient religions which demanded human sacrifice, faiths which spring from some irrational belief (rooted in theology or metaphysics) in the existence of vast and menacing powers, once the objects of blind religious worship, then, with the decay of primitive faith, degraded to becoming terms of political rhetoric. The dogmas of such religions declare that mere invocation of certain formulae, certain symbols, renders what would normally be regarded as crimes or lunacies—murder, torture, the humiliation of defenceless human bodies—not only permissible, but often laudable. Against this Herzen advances his own positive beliefs: that man is, within narrow but discernible limits, free; that he is neither the impotent plaything of natural forces, nor a trivial unit in a uniform mass of historical raw material intended by some unknown deity for consumption by the great historical process—the Hegelian 'slaughter-bench of history'—and consequently dedicated to self-immolation, that thereby the march of the spirit might be rendered more glorious. This is the doctrine at the heart of German historical romanticism as interpreted both by the reactionary right and by the revolutionary left; and indeed has formed the content of much subsequent German thought and art, with its recurrent emphasis upon the supreme value of the death and transfiguration, if need be, of entire peoples and civilizations in wars and revolutions and other forms of terrible, but inevitable, and thereby sanctified, cataclysm.

Herzen rejected this as nothing but a sadistic mythology possessing no moral justification, founded on no empirical evidence. He believed that morality was not a fixed, objective, eternal code, a set of immutable commandments which human beings were merely required to discern and obey, whether they were ordained by a personal deity or were found in 'nature' or 'the logic of history'. He maintained that men create their own morality; that, animated by that egoism without which there is no vitality and no creative activity, the individual is responsible for his own choices, and cannot plead the *alibi* of either nature or history for failing even to try to bring about that which he considers, for whatever reason, to be good, or just, or delightful, or beautiful, or true. This denial on his part that it was, in principle, possible to formulate general and eternal moral rules, made without a trace of Byronic self-dramatization or Nietzschean hyperbole, is a doctrine that is not often encountered in the nineteenth century; indeed, in its full extent, not till well into our own, where it forms a bridge between empiricists endowed with moral imagination and existentialists who have something genuinely intelligible to say. It hits both right and left: against romantic historians, against

Hegel, and to some degree against Kant, against utilitarians and against supermen, against Tolstoy and against the religion of art, against 'scientific' and 'evolutionary' ethics, against all the churches. It is empirical and naturalistic, recognizes values that are absolute for those who hold them, as well as change, and is overawed neither by determinism nor by socialism. And it is very independent. Herzen attacked with particular indignation those who appealed to general principles to justify savage cruelties and defended the slaughter of thousands to-day by the promise that millions would thereby be made happy in some invisible future, condoning unheard-of miseries and injustices in the name of some overwhelming but remote felicity. This attitude Herzen regards as nothing but a pernicious delusion, perhaps a deliberate deception; for the distant ends may never be realized, while the agonies and sufferings and crimes of the present remain only too real; and since we know so little of the future, and possess no means of accurate prediction, to affirm the opposite and seek to condone the effects of our brutal acts by holding out such hollow promises is either lunacy or fraud. We cannot tell whether the millions will ever achieve the happy condition we have so confidently guaranteed to them; but what we do know is that thousands will perish, unheard, to-day. Distant ends are for Herzen not ends at all, but a monstrous delusion—ends must be closer at hand, 'the labourer's daily wage, or pleasure in the work performed'.

Inhabitants of the twentieth century scarcely need to be reminded of the tyranny of the great altruistic systems; of liberators who crush, of 'the arithmetical pantheism of universal suffrage' and 'superstitious faith in republics' on the one hand, or the brutal arrogance of minorities on the other. Herzen, however, was writing a century ago, in a time of mounting democratic eloquence, when the enemy was cold-hearted individualism, or clerical and dynastic despotism, and against them there rose the vast, visionary utopias of socialists and Catholics and Hegelians and positivists and many another among the great metaphysical and religious system-builders of the nineteenth century. This was the dominant current, and Herzen resisted it both intellectually and emotionally, because it seemed to him to threaten individual liberty. As a thinker in the Western tradition (and, despite his paeans to the Russian peasant, Herzen's populism, like Tolstoy's, derives from Rousseau rather than native soil), he is enlightened and sceptical. He belongs to the tradition of Erasmus and Montaigne, Bayle and Fontenelle, Voltaire and Constant, Humboldt and the English philosophic radicals, of all those who protest against despotism wherever they find it, not merely in the oppression of priests or kings or dictators, but in the dehumanizing effect of those vast cosmologies which minimize the role of the individual, curb his freedom, repress his desire for self-expression, and order him to humble himself before the great laws and institutions of the universe, immovable, omnipotent and everlasting, in whose sight free human choice is but a pathetic illusion.

All such systems seemed to Herzen equally spurious. In *From the Other Shore* he attacks the meanness and enviousness of the bourgeoisie which crushes everything original, independent or open, as he attacks clerical or military reaction, or the hatred of freedom and barbarous brutality of the masses. He has a sense of impending doom no less vivid than Marx or Burckhardt, but, whereas in the writings of both Marx and other Hegelian visionaries there is an unmistakable note of sardonic joy in the very thought of vast and destructive powers unchained against the bad old world, Herzen is free from the desire to prostrate himself before the mere spectacle of irresistible power; he is free from contempt for or hatred of weakness as such, and from the romantic pessimism which is at the heart of the nihilism and fascism that were to come. If communism—the revolt of the masses—is ever allowed to sweep across Europe, it will be 'dreadful, bloody, unjust, swift', and, in the name of the blood and tears of the oppressed, will mow down all that civilized men hold dear. But, unlike the apocalyptic prophets of his time, Herzen thinks this cataclysm neither inevitable nor glorious. When he warns his friends against the 'Phrygian cap' or the red flag of the masses as being no less murderous than the 'bloodstained sword' of the ruling class, he does so not out of romantic despair, but with a positive purpose, because he thinks that knowledge, reason, will-power, courage, can avert the danger, and alter the course of mankind. It may, of course, be too late; Europe—the West—may well be going under; must Russia, too, be submerged in the tidal wave?

The clearest exposition of Herzen's hopes and fears for his country is contained in the open letter, published in this volume, addressed to the celebrated French historian, Jules Michelet. A friend of the great poet Mickiewicz—'the martyr of Europe', the greatest of all the victims of Russian oppression—and of his fellow exiles from Poland, Michelet had written passionately denouncing the Russians as inhuman savages unfit to associate with European nations. Herzen replied temperately, with genuine sympathy for the Poles, and expounded, in answer to Michelet, some of those optimistic, and indeed utopian, notions on which as he grew progressively more pessimistic about the prospects of the Western world, he had fixed his hopes. He saw salvation in the communal organization of the Russian peasants, and wrote eloquent pages about their generous and spontaneous Russian character uncontaminated by the corroding doubts and moral squalor of the Western world in decline. He had somehow persuaded himself that the uncorrupted Russian peasantry, with its natural socialism, would of itself suffice to solve the 'greatest problem of the century'—how to reconcile the claims of individual liberty with the demands of an inevitably more and more centralized authority, how to preserve personal life, without 'atomizing' society, the central dilemma which 'the Western world has thus far failed to solve'. Collectivized production together with the preservation of the rights and freedoms of individual persons—rights and freedoms for which neither Marx nor Cabet nor Louis Blanc had shown the least sympathy—that is the answer with which the Russian peasant will astonish the world. True, the peasant commune had not been sufficient to save Russia from the nightmare of Byzantium, or the Tartar yoke, or the big stick of German officialdom, or the Tsar's knout; but armed with Western scientific techniques, the unbroken Russian *moujik* will yet teach the world a great lesson in social organization. Russian populism, whether sentimental or realistic, owes more to the ungrounded optimism with which Herzen comforted himself than to any other single source.

Herzen struck impartially in all directions, and so was duly condemned by both sides: by the right wing as a subverter of Church and State; by the left, particularly by the new young revolutionaries in Russia, as a self-indulgent sceptic, too rich, too civilized, too elegant, too much a gentleman, too comfortably established in the West to understand the harsh realities of the Russian situation, and dangerous, too, because prone to sound a note of disillusion, even of cynicism, and so to weaken the sinews of the revolution—liable to become ironical and, worse still, entertaining, at a time when serious men must decide to commit themselves to one side or the other without so much fastidious regard to their private consciences and scruples. Herzen replied by saying that organized hooliganism and nihilism solved nothing; and in one of his last writings drew his own vignette of the 'new men': the new generation would say to the old: '"you are hypocrites, we will be cynics; you spoke like moralists, we shall speak like scoundrels; you were civil to your superiors, rude to your inferiors; we shall be rude to everyone; you bow without feeling respect, we shall push and jostle and make no apologies . . ."'.

On the whole, it is Herzen's totalitarian opponents both of the right and of the left that have triumphed. And it is a singular curiosity of history (of a kind which Herzen himself delighted to describe with incomparable malice and wit) that, on the strength of laudatory references to him by Lenin, this enemy of authority, who was, perhaps, the most devastating, as he certainly was the most understanding, opponent of the many communisms of his day—the enemy of all dogma, who declared that *salus populi* was as vicious a cry as *lèse majesté*, that no ideal at which one was forbidden to smile was worth anything at all—it is a strange irony that Herzen, who had no love for Marx and the 'Marxids' (as he called them) either personally or politically, and was denounced most bitterly by them, should find himself canonized in his native country to-day as one of the sacrosanct founders of the new way of life. The 'nihilists' of the '60s and the socialist writers of a later date who attack him for his liberal inclinations are a good deal more honest and consistent. Their suspicions turned out to be valid enough. For Herzen does like the style and colour of free human beings; best of all he likes fire, originality, aesthetic feeling, even when it is found in oligarchies and aristocracies. He has no affinity with the mass of the oppressed as such, only indignation and a desire for justice. The qualities that he loves best are those which they too seldom possess—imagination, spontaneity, humanity, civilized feelings, natural generosity, courage, wide horizons, instinctive knowledge of what individual freedom is, and hatred of all forms of slavery or arbitrary rule, or human humiliation and degradation. And he extols these virtues wherever he finds them, even in the camp of the oppressors; and rejects political formulae and generalizations however deeply sanctified by the martyrdom of fighters for a cause which he called his own. He declares over and over again that words and ideas offer no substitute for experience, that life teems with exceptions, and upsets the best made rules and systems. But in his case this attitude led not to detachment or quietism—to the tolerant conservatism of a Hume or a Bagehot—but was allied to an impatient, passionate, rebellious temperament, which made him the rarest of characters, a revolutionary without fanaticism, a man ready for violent change, never in the name of abstract principles, but only of actual misery and injustice, of concrete conditions so bad that men were morally not permitted—and knew that they were not permitted—to let them exist.

Starting from this kind of clear-sighted empiricism, which was influenced by the imaginative sweep of Hegel but rejected his metaphysical dogmas, Herzen gave expression to theses original enough to be rediscovered only in our own time: that the great traditional problems which perennially agitate men's minds have no general solutions; that all genuine questions are of necessity specific, intelligible only in specific contexts; that general problems, such as 'What is *the* end (or *the* meaning) of life?' or 'What makes all events in nature occur as they do?' or 'What is *the* pattern of human history?' are not answerable in principle, not because they are too difficult for our poor, finite intellects, but because the questions themselves are misconceived, because ends, patterns, meanings, causes, differ with the situation and outlook and needs of the questioner, and can be correctly and clearly formulated only if these are understood. It is Herzen's grasp of this fact that made him the forerunner of much twentieth-century thought, and marks him as a man with a quality akin to philosophical genius.

Herzen never forgot, as some of his most inspired fellow revolutionaries often did, that actual human beings, and specific problems, can be lost sight of in the midst of statistical generalizations. In his discussion of what men live by, there occurs the smallest proportion of abstraction and generalization, and the highest proportion of vivid, three-dimensional, 'rounded' perception of actual character, authentic human beings with real needs, seeking attainable human ends, set in circumstances which can be visualized. And in the course of his analyses he uses the Russian language with a virtuosity to which no translation is ever likely to do complete justice. It was not for nothing that Tolstoy admired his writings and Dostoevsky recognized him as a poet.[1] Essayist,

[1] In his *Diary of a Writer* Dostoevsky expresses his deep admiration for *From the Other Shore* and tells the story of how he personally

agitator, publicist, revolutionary, philosopher, novelist, author of at least one work of genius, Herzen's position in the history not merely of Russian literature, but of Russia itself (as his friend, the critic Belinsky, had prophesied when they were both still in their early thirties), is to-day unique and secure. But he deserves to be read beyond the borders of Russia, if only for his moral and political ideas. Many of his predictions were falsified by events, and his practical remedies, since they were not, and perhaps could not have been, applied, can be written off as utopian. But his central perceptions remain as fresh and arresting to-day as when they were first uttered by him more than a hundred years ago, and their relevance to our times seems even greater than to his own.

ISAIAH BERLIN

---

congratulated Herzen on it, saying that what had particularly impressed him was the fact that the author's opponent in the dialogue was not a man of straw, but a formidable controversialist who managed to drive Herzen into awkward corners—'Ah, but, of course, that is the whole point,' Herzen replied.

BIBLIOGRAPHICAL NOTE

From the Other Shore in its present form consists mainly of articles written by Alexander Herzen in Russian in 1847–9, in Paris, for the benefit of his friends in Moscow, to whom he sent them in successive parts. Some were contributed to French, German and Italian journals; the first full edition appeared in German under the title *Vom Anderen Ufer*, printed in Zurich in 1849 and published by Hoffman and Campe, Hamburg, in 1850. No author's name is given, though on the title-page the book is said to be 'aus dem Russischen Manuskript'; one of the articles it contains is signed 'Barbar', the other 'Ein Russe'. It was in fact, according to the author, translated by himself and F. Kapp, to whom Herzen dictated it from the Russian original; Herzen's then friend the German poet Georg Herwegh helped to correct and edit the translation. The second edition appeared in Russian under the title *S Togo Berega*, in London in 1855; it was published by Herzen himself under his well-known pseudonym 'Iskander' (the Arabic version of 'Alexander'). This edition was the first to include the dedication to his son Alexander and the author's introduction, though Herzen sent the address entitled 'Farewell' (dated 1 March 1849 in the 1855 text) to his Moscow friends in August 1849 under the title 'Addio'. The third edition, revised by the author, but almost identical with the second, appeared also in London in Russian, in 1858. Apart from a lithographed version published clandestinely in Moscow in the '50s, the next authoritative edition is the French translation, *De l'Autre Rive*, prepared by Herzen's son Alexander, and published in Geneva in 1870.

The German edition contained 'Before the Storm', 'Vixerunt!', 'Consolatio', 'After the Storm' and 'Year LVII of the Republic, One and Indivisible', as well as two Open Letters, the first addressed to Georg Herwegh, the second to Mazzini, which did not reappear in Russian editions (they were later published separately) on the ground that they were intended primarily for foreigners. Accordingly the first complete edition is the Russian edition of 1855, incorporating some articles previously printed elsewhere, i.e. 'Epilogue 1849' (*New York Abend-Zeitung*, New York, 1850; *Deutsche Monatsschrift für Politik, Wissenschaft, Kunst und Leben*, Stuttgart, 1850 No. 12), 'Omnia Mea Mecum Porto' (*Deutsche Monatsschrift*, 1850 No. 8), and 'Donoso-Cortes' (*La Voix du Peuple*, Paris, No. 167, March 18th, 1850, signed 'Is . . . . . r, Docteur en théologie'). Large parts of 'After the Storm' are incorporated in Volume IV of Herzen's memoirs. The earliest authoritative text is that contained in M. K. Lemke's standard edition of Herzen's works. It appears in Volume V (dated St Petersburg 1915). As the Tsarist censorship was in force at this period, Lemke added a list of excised passages after the February Revolution of 1917, when restrictions were lifted. In the present volume the translator has followed the text of *From the Other Shore* contained in the Soviet edition[1] in

[1]The new edition of Herzen's Collected Works and Letters published by the Academy of Sciences of the USSR, which largely supersedes Lemke's edition, had not in July 1955 reached works written outside Russia. This definitive edition is now complete, in thirty volumes: *Sobraniye Sochineniy v Tridtsati Tomakh* (Moscow 1954–66). *From the Other Shore* and *The Russian People and Socialism* constitute Volume VI and part of Volume VII. This excellent work of scholarship contains extensive bibliographical data as well as lists of variant readings and copious introductions and notes.

two volumes of Herzen's philosophical works published under the imprint of Ogiz, Moscow, 1946, which virtually reproduces Lemke's text with the excisions restored. There are minor variations between the Lemke edition and the various editions published outside Russia before the Revolution, and in the Soviet Union after it.

There are some interesting articles relating to this book in the various numbers of Kolatschek's periodical *Deutsche Monatsschrift für Politik, Wissenschaft, Kunst und Leben* for 1850. It is to these that Herzen refers in the introduction.

Research among Herzen's manuscripts has so far failed to reveal the original manuscript of the work, although a copy of 'After the Storm' annotated in Herzen's own hand exists in Moscow.

The Russian People and Socialism was published originally in a much shorter form under the title 'Le Peuple Russe, Lettre à M. J. Michelet, Professeur au Collège de France' in *L'Avènement du Peuple* (Paris, No. 63, November 19th, 1851), and was signed by Herzen. In this journal Michelet had published his 'Légendes Démocratiques', and Herzen's essay is a reply to one of them, 'Pologne et Russie. Légende de Kosciusko' (August 28th–September 17th, 1851). The first full edition was printed at the Imprimerie Canis Frères, Nice, at the end of 1851, with the imprint 'A. Franck, Librairie Etrangère, Paris, 1852', and was signed 'Iscander (A. Herzen)'. It was republished, again in French, under the title *Le Peuple Russe et le Socialisme. Lettre à Monsieur J. Michelet, Professeur au Collège de France*, in Jersey in 1855; to this edition Herzen contributed an introduction explaining that the first edition circulated only in Piedmont and Switzerland, because the French police seized the entire edition at Marseilles and 'in a strange fit of absent-mindedness failed to return it'. In that same year an English translation by W. J. Linton appeared in his periodical *The English Republic.* Linton then reprinted this translation as a separate pamphlet under the title 'The Russian People and their Socialism, a Letter to M. J. Michelet' at the private press he had established at Brantwood, Coniston, Windermere (later Ruskin's house). The first Russian edition (supervised by the author but without naming the translator from the French original) appeared in London (Trübner, 1858). From then onwards *The Russian People and Socialism* has appeared in all the collected editions of Herzen's works. It has also been included in some versions of Herzen's memoirs (including Constance Garnett's translation).

The review in the London *Leader* (No. 512) and Proudhon's letter to Chojecki of November 25th, 1851 (*Correspondence de P-J Proudhon*, Paris 1875, Vol. IV, p. 130) are both worth reading.

Herzen's greatest work, his memoirs, *Byloye i Dumy* (*Past and Reflections*), is available in English in the complete translation by Constance Garnett, revised by Humphrey Higgens, under the title *My Past and Thoughts* (4 volumes, London 1968; abridged and edited in one volume by Dwight Macdonald, London 1974), and its first two parts in the translation by J. D. Duff (*Childhood, Youth and Exile*, Oxford 1979). Duff's translation is among the best renderings of Russian prose into English to be found anywhere. Two essays on Herzen by Isaiah Berlin appear as introductions to these translations.

CHRONOLOGICAL TABLE
OF EVENTS 1847–9

1847

Campaign for political reform led by *Le National* (edited by Marrast) and *La Réforme* (edited by Ledru-Rollin).

1848

February 22. Disturbances in Paris over prohibition of political banquets.

February 23. Resignation of Guizot. Rioting in Paris.

February 24. Abdication of Louis-Phillipe. Proclamation of Republic and establishment of Provisional Government (Dupont de l'Eure, Arago, Lamartine, Ledru-Rollin, Crémieux, Marie, Garnier-Pagès).

February 27. Establishment of National Workshops for unemployed.

March 5. Proclamation of universal male suffrage and secret ballot.

March 16. Reactionary demonstration of *bonnets à poil.*

March 17. Large left-wing counter-demonstration.

April 23. Election of Constituent Assembly.

May 4. Meeting of Constituent Assembly.

May 9–10. Establishment of Executive Committee (Arago, Garnier-Pagès, Marie, Lamartine, Ledru-Rollin).

May 15. Demonstration in favour of liberation of Poland led by Barbès and Blanqui, suppressed by National Guard. Flight or imprisonment of extreme left-wing leaders.

Emergence of three parties:

(i) *Réunion de Palais National*, or moderate republicans under Marrast.

(ii). *Réunion de la Montagne*, or radical republicans under Ledru-Rollin.
(iii). *Party of Order.*

June 21. Decree restricting National Workshops.

June 23–7. Revolt of the June days in Paris, suppressed in bloody fighting by Cavaignac aided by National Guard from the provinces. Repression of left-wing movement. Cavaignac at the head of moderate republican government.

September 17. By-elections. Louis-Napoleon Bonaparte elected by five departments.

November 4. Proclamation of Constitution of Second Republic.

December 10. Election of Louis-Napoleon Bonaparte as President by 5½ million votes to 1½ million for Cavaignac. Appointment of ministry under Odilon Barrot, largely composed of former Orleanists.

1849

March 7–April 2. Bourges trial of leaders of demonstration of May 15.

April 24. French expeditionary force under Oudinot despatched to Rome.

May 18. Election of Legislative Assembly. Party of Order obtains 500 seats out of 700. Emergence of new radical republican movement under Ledru-Rollin.

May 25. Final dissolution of Constituent Assembly.

May 26. First meeting of new Legislative Assembly.

June 13. Fruitless attempt at republican rising in Paris. Flight of Ledru-Rollin. Systematic repression of all surviving radical opinion and activity.

June 30. Oudinot overthrows Roman Republic.

October 1. Formation of Presidential ministry under Louis-Napoleon.

FROM THE OTHER SHORE

AUTHOR'S INTRODUCTION

TO MY SON ALEXANDER

My friend Sasha,

I dedicate this book to you, because I have never written, and probably shall never write, anything better, because I love this book as a monument to a struggle in which I have sacrificed much, but not the courage of knowledge; and because, ultimately, I have no fear whatever of putting into your young hands this, at times insolent, protest of an independent individual against an obsolete, slavish and spurious set of ideas, against absurd idols, which belong to another age and which linger on meaninglessly among us, a nuisance to some, a terror to others.

I do not wish to deceive you; you must know the truth as I know it; may you enter into *this* truth not through agonizing error and crushing disappointment, but simply as an inheritance.

In your life there will be other questions, other conflicts . . . there will be no lack of toil and suffering. You are only fifteen, and already have experienced some terrible shocks.

Do not look for solutions in this book—there are none; in general modern man has no solutions. What is solved is finished, and the coming upheaval is only beginning.

We do not build, we destroy; we do not proclaim a new revelation, we eliminate the old lie. Modern man, that melancholy *Pontifex Maximus*, only builds a bridge—it will be for the unknown man of the future to pass over it. You may be there to see him. . . . But do not, I beg, remain on *this shore*. . . . Better to perish with the revolution than to seek refuge in the almshouse of reaction.

The religion of the coming revolution is the only one that I bequeath to you. It has no paradise to offer, no rewards, except your own awareness, except conscience. . . . When the time comes go and preach it amongst us *at home*; my language was once loved there and perhaps they will remember me.

. . . I bless you on your way in the name of human reason, personal liberty and fraternity!

YOUR FATHER

RICHMOND HOUSE,
TWICKENHAM,
January 1st, 1855

I have added three articles published in journals and intended for the second edition, which the German censorship banned; these three articles are *Epilogue*, *Omnia mea mecum porto*, and *Donoso-Cortes*. I have put them in place of a short article on Russia written for foreigners.

A. I. H.

Vom Andern Ufer is my first book published in the West; the articles that compose it were written in Russian in 1848 and 1849. I dictated them myself, in German, to a young writer, F. Kapp.[1]

There is much in it that is no longer new. Five terrible years have taught something to the most stubborn, the most unrepentant sinners of *our* shore. In the early part of 1850 my book made a great stir in Germany; it was furiously praised and abused, and while there appeared more than flattering reviews by such men as Julius Froebel,[2] Jacoby,[3] Falmereier,[4] other talented and conscientious writers angrily attacked it.

I was accused of preaching despondency, of having no knowledge of the people, of *dépit amoureux* towards the Revolution, of lack of respect for democracy, for the masses, for Europe. . . .

December the 2nd[5] spoke louder than I.

[1]Friedrich Kapp (1824–84), Prussian judicial official who became a left-wing agitator and journalist in 1848. Left Germany after rising of September 1848 and travelled with Herzen. Returned to Germany in autumn 1849 and took part in the Baden rising. Emigrated to America 1855 and became an American citizen. Wrote historical and sociological works. Returned to Germany and became a member of Reichstag, as National Liberal 1872–77, Progressive 1881–84.

[2]Julius Froebel (1806–93), nephew of the great educationalist. Radical politician and member of the Frankfurt Assembly, 1848. Emigrated to America after failure of the revolution; returned in 1857; German consul in Smyrna and Algiers.

[3]Johann Jacoby (1805–1877), later member of Social Democratic party.

[4]Philipp Jakob Falmereier (1791–1860), German historian and traveller. Radical member of the Frankfurt Assembly, fled into exile and shortly after retired from public life.

[5]Coup d'état of Louis Bonaparte in 1851.

In 1852 I met in London the most sharp-witted of my opponents, Solger [1]; he was packing in order to leave for America straight away; in Europe, it seemed, there was nothing for him *to do*. 'Circumstances seem to have convinced you,' I remarked, 'that I was not altogether mistaken?' 'I didn't need all that,' replied Solger, laughing amiably, 'to realize that I was writing sheer nonsense at the time.'

In spite of this charming admission, the general consensus of opinion, the abiding impression went, if anything, against me. Does not this feeling of irritation indicate the imminence of danger, fear of the future, the desire to conceal one's weakness, a peevish, petrified old age? . . . But where there is danger there is hope! It is the peculiar destiny of the Russians to see further than their neighbours, to see in darker colours and to express their opinions boldly—Russians, those 'mutes' as Michelet once called them.

This is what one of our compatriots wrote long before:

'Who, more than we, extolled the virtues of the eighteenth century, the light of philosophy, the softening of manners, the universal spread of public spirit, the close and friendly ties binding the peoples, the mildness of rulers? . . . Though a few black clouds still appeared on humanity's horizon, yet hope's bright ray gilded their tips . . . we considered the end of our century would mark the end of the chief ills of mankind, and thought to see in it the fusion of theory and practice, of thought and action . . . where now is this most comforting system?

'It destroyed itself in the making; the eighteenth century is ending and the miserable philanthropist takes but two strides to measure his grave, to lay himself down in it with

[1] Reinhold Solger (d. 1866). Prussian littérateur and radical. Made Herzen's acquaintance in the house of Georg Herwegh in autumn 1847. In 1848 was in England: returned to Germany to support the revolutionary cause. Emigrated first to Switzerland, then to England, finally to America.

his heart lacerated and betrayed, and close his eyes for ever.

'Who could have thought of it, expected it, foreseen it? Where are the men we loved? Where is the fruit of learning and wisdom? Age of enlightenment—I know thee not; in blood and fire, amidst slaughter and destruction I know thee not.

'The *misosophers* triumph. "Here are the fruits of your enlightenment," they say, "here the fruits of your learning; let philosophy perish."—And the poor wretch deprived of his country, the poor wretch without home, father, son or friend, repeats: "Let it perish!" Bloodshed cannot last for ever; I am certain that the hand that wields the sword will grow weary; sulphur and saltpetre will run dry in the bowels of the earth, soon or late the thunder will cease, silence will reign—but what order of silence will it be?—And what if it be dead, cold, gloomy? . . .

'The downfall of learning seems to me not only possible but even inevitable, even imminent. . . . When it falls, when its magnificent edifice crumbles, when the beneficent sacred flame dies down—what then? I am appalled, my heart trembles. Suppose that a few sparks are preserved beneath the ashes; suppose that there are men who find them, and with them light their quiet solitary huts—but what will become of the world?

'I cover my face with my hands!

'Can it be that the human race in our time has attained the highest possible degree of enlightenment and must again sink back into barbarism, and again, little by little, rise therefrom, like the stone of Sisyphus, which, having been rolled up to the top of the hill, by its own weight rolls down and is again rolled up to the top by the hands of the everlasting toiler?—most melancholy prospect!

'It seems to me now as though the ancient chronicles themselves prove the probability of this opinion. We barely know the names of the ancient Asiatic peoples and

Kingdoms, but some historical fragments seem to show that these people were not barbarians. . . . Kingdoms crumbled, peoples vanished, from their dust were born new tribes. They were born in twilight, in the trembling mist. They had a childhood, they learned, they grew famous. Perhaps aeons sank into eternity and more than once did the light of day break in the minds of men and more than once did night darken their souls before even the light of Egypt shone forth.

'The enlightenment of Egypt joins hands with that of Greece, the Romans learnt in the same great school.

'And what followed this brilliant epoch? Many centuries of barbarism.

'Slowly the dense darkness was dispersed, slowly the light broke through the thick gloom. And at last the sun blazed forth; good and credulous humanitarians reasoning from triumph to triumph perceived the approaching goal of perfection and in joyful ecstasy exclaimed: "The shore!", but suddenly the sky was overcast and the fate of mankind hidden in the storm clouds. Oh posterity! What destiny awaits thee!

'Sometimes when unbearable sadness grips my heart, I fall on my knees and stretch out my hands to the Invisible. . . . No answer!—my head sinks to my breast.

'Eternal movement in the self-same circle. Eternal reiteration, eternal alternation of day and night, night and day, one drop of joy and a sea of bitter tears. My friend! What am I to live for? Or you? Or any of us? What did our forefathers live for? What will posterity live for?

'My spirit is heavy, weak and sorrowful!'

These tormented lines, fiery and full of tears, were written towards the end of the '90s—by *N. M. Karamzin.*[1]

[1]*Mélodore to Philalèthe* (1795). Nicolai Michailovitch Karamzin (1765–1826). Father of modern Russian historiography. The nobility of his prose style and the distinction of his personality secured a unique position for him in Russia at the beginning of the

The introduction to the Russian text consisted of a few words addressed to friends in Russia. I did not deem it necessary to repeat them in the German edition—here they are:

FAREWELL

PARIS
March 1st, 1849

Our parting will last for a long time yet—perhaps for ever. At the present moment I do not wish to return—whether it will be possible later I do not know. You have been waiting for me, you are still waiting, so I must give you an explanation. If there is anyone to whom I am obliged to account for my absence, for my actions, it is certainly you, my friends.

An unconquerable revulsion and a strong inner voice of prophecy do not permit me to cross the frontier of Russia, especially now, when autocracy, infuriated and frightened by everything that is happening in Europe, strangles with redoubled severity every intellectual movement, and brutally cuts off sixty million souls from the rest of mankind which is gaining its freedom, deflecting the last light which falls feebly on a few of them with its black iron hand caked with the blood of Poland. No, my friends, I cannot cross the border of this kingdom of darkness, lawlessness, silent death, mysterious disappearances, gagged and tortured prisoners. I shall wait until that time when the weary rulers weakened by vain efforts and by the resistance that they have provoked, recognize *something* worthy of respect in the Russian man.

Do not, I beg you, make a mistake: it is not happiness, not distraction, not rest, not even personal safety that I have found here; indeed, I do not know who could find in

nineteenth century. What makes this passage remarkable is its difference of tone from the *bien pensant* conservatism of the celebrated History of Russia. In his later years Karamzin became a convinced monarchist and the admired adviser of Tsar Alexander I, and threw his influence against social and political reform.

Europe to-day happiness or rest, rest in the midst of an earthquake, happiness in the midst of a desperate struggle.

You saw sadness expressed in every line of my letters; life here is very hard, venomous malignity mingles with love, bile with tears, feverish anxiety infects the whole organism, the time of former illusions and hopes has passed. I believe in nothing here, except in a handful of people, a few ideas, and the fact that one cannot arrest movement; I see the inevitable doom of old Europe and feel no pity for anything that now exists, neither the peaks of its culture nor its institutions. . . . I love nothing in this world except that which it persecutes, I respect nothing except that which it kills—and I stay . . . stay to suffer doubly, to suffer my own personal anguish and that of this world; which will perish, perhaps, to the sound of thunder and destruction towards which it is racing at full steam. . . . Why then do I stay?

I stay because the struggle is *here*, because despite the blood and tears it is here that social problems are being decided, because it is here that suffering is painful, sharp, but *articulate*. The struggle is open, no one hides. Woe to the vanquished, but they are not vanquished without a struggle, nor deprived of speech before they can utter a word; the violence inflicted is great, but the protest is loud; the fighters often march to the galleys, chained hand and foot, but with heads uplifted, with free speech. Where the word has not perished, neither has the deed. For the sake of this open struggle, for this free speech, this right to be heard—I stay here; for its sake I give up everything; I give up you for it, a portion of my heritage and perhaps shall give my life in the ranks of an energetic minority of 'the persecuted but undefeated'.

For the sake of this freedom of speech, I have broken, or, better still, suppressed for a while my ties of blood with the people in whom I found so much response both to the bright and to the dark side of my soul, whose song and speech are my song and speech, and I stay among a people in whose life I am in deep sympathy only with the bitter tears of the proletariat and the desperate courage of its friends.

This decision has cost me dear . . . you know me . . . and you will believe me. I have stifled the inner pain; I have lived through the painful struggle and I have made my decision, not like an angry youth, but like a man who has thought over what he is doing . . . how much he has to lose . . . for months I have been calculating and pondering and vacillating, and have finally sacrificed everything to:

Human Dignity and Free Speech

The consequences are no affair of mine; they are not in my power, they are rather in the power of some arbitrary whim which has gone so far as to draw a capricious circle not only round our words but round our very steps. It was in my power not to obey—and I did not obey.

To obey against one's convictions when there is a possibility of not obeying—is immoral. Passive obedience becomes almost impossible. I have witnessed two upheavals, I have lived too long as a free man to allow myself to be chained again; I have lived through popular disturbances, I have become accustomed to free speech and I cannot accept serfdom again, not even for the sake of suffering with you. If it had been necessary to restrain oneself for the common cause, perhaps one might have found the strength to do so; but where at this moment is our common cause? At home you have no soil on which a free man can stand. How after this can you summon us? . . . If it were to battle —yes, then we would come: but to obscure martyrdom, to sterile silence, to obedience—no, under no circumstances. Demand anything of me, but do not demand duplicity, do not force me again to play at being a loyal subject; respect the free man in me.

The liberty of the individual is the greatest thing of all, it is *on this and on this alone* that the true will of the people can develop. Man must respect liberty in himself, and he must esteem it in himself no less than in his neighbour, than in the entire nation. If you are convinced of that, then you will agree that to remain here is my right, my duty; it is the only protest that an individual can make amongst us; he must offer up this sacrifice to his human dignity. If you call my withdrawal an escape and will forgive me only out of your love, this will mean that you yourselves are not wholly free.

I know all the answers that can be made from the point of view of romantic patriotism and formal civil responsibility, but I cannot allow these antiquated attitudes. I have outlived them, left them behind, and it is precisely against them that I am fighting. These *réchauffé* remnants of the Roman and Christian heritage are the greatest obstacles to the establishment of true ideas of freedom, ideas that are healthy, clear, mature. Fortunately, in Europe, custom and a long process of development partly counterbalance these absurd theories and absurd laws. The people who live here are living on a soil fertilized by two civilizations; the path traversed by their ancestors for the past two and a half thousand years was not in vain, many human virtues have developed independently of the external organization and the official order.

Even in the worst periods of European history, we encounter some respect for the individual, some recognition of independence, some rights conceded to talent and genius. Vile as were the German rulers of that time, Spinoza was not sentenced to transportation, Lessing was not flogged or conscripted. This respect not merely for material but also for moral force, this unquestioning recognition of the individual—is one of the great human principles in European life.

In Europe a man who lives abroad has never been considered a criminal, nor one who emigrates to America a traitor.

We have nothing similar. With us the individual has always been crushed, absorbed, he has never even tried to emerge. Free speech with us has always been considered insolence, independence, subversion; man was engulfed in the State, dissolved in the community. The revolution of Peter the Great replaced the obsolete squirearchy of Russia —with a European bureaucracy; everything that could be copied from the Swedish and German codes, everything that could be taken over from the free municipalities of Holland into our half-communal, half-absolutist country, was taken over; but the unwritten, the moral check on power, the instinctive recognition of the rights of man, of the rights of thought, of truth, could not be and were not imported.

With us slavery increased with education; the State grew and improved but the individual reaped nothing from it; on the contrary, the stronger the State, the weaker the individual. European forms of administration and justice, of military and civil organization, developed with us into a kind of monstrous and inescapable despotism.

Were it not that Russia was so vast, that the alien system of power was so chaotically established, so incompetently administered, one might have said without exaggeration that no human being with any sense of his own dignity could live in Russia.

Pampered authority, never meeting with any opposition, reached at times a degree of unbridled violence that has no equal in history. You can take its measure from the stories about that master of his trade, Tsar Paul. Take away the capricious, the fantastic element in Paul, and you will see that he is not original at all, that the principle that inspired him is not only the same as that of every tsar, but of every governor, every policeman, every landowner. The intoxication of arbitrary power has overcome every single one of the fourteen grades in the famous hierarchy.[1] Every act of power, every relation of superior to inferior, reveals a brazen shamelessness, an arrogant display of moral indifference, the insulting conviction that the individual will endure anything: triple recruitment, the law about foreign passports, flogging in the Institute of Engineers. Just as Little Russia submitted to serfdom in the eighteenth century, so in the end the whole of Russia came to believe that men could be sold and re-sold and no one, not even those who were being sold, ever asked on what legal basis this was done. With us authority feels freer, more self-confident than in Turkey or Persia, nothing restrains it, no past of any kind; it has repudiated its own past and is not concerned with that of Europe. It has no respect for national principles, it knows no universal culture, and it fights against the present.

In the past the government at least felt shame before its neighbours, learnt from them. Now it feels called upon itself to act as an example to all oppressors: now it is itself the mentor.

We have seen, you and I, the most terrible development of imperial power. We grew up under the terror, under the black wings of the secret police, in its very claws; we were crippled by its merciless oppression; and just managed to survive. But is this enough? Is it not time to untie our hands and tongues for action, to set an example, is it not time to awaken the slumbering consciousness of the people? But can one do this if one speaks in whispers, in obscure hints, at a time when shouts and plain speech are barely heard? Brave, open acts are necessary. December the 14th [2] shook young Russia so strongly because it took place on St Isaac's

[1] In his 'table of ranks' Peter the Great laid down a hierarchy of fourteen grades through which all members of the Russian gentry were entitled to pass. Promotion was solely by service to the state.

[2] Old style version of December 25th, the date of the outbreak of the famous Decembrist rising of 1825.

Square. Now not only a public square, but the printed word, the professorial chair—everything has become impossible in Russia. All that remains is individual work in retirement or individual protest from afar.

I remain here not only because I should find it abhorrent after crossing the frontier to wear handcuffs again, but because I want to work. To sit with hands folded is possible anywhere; here I have no other task but *ours*.

He who for more than twenty years has carried in his heart one single thought, who has suffered for it, and lived by it, and known many a prison and many a banishment, and owes it the best moments of his life, the brightest friendships, will not abandon it, will not subject it to the demands of expediency, to the geographical degree of latitude and longitude; quite the contrary: here I am more useful, here I am your uncensored voice, your free press, your chance representative.

All this seems new and strange only to us; actually there is nothing unusual about it. In every country, at the beginning of an upheaval, while thought is still feeble and material power unbridled, men of energy and devotion withdraw, their free speech rings out from the distance and this very *distance* gives their words strength and authority because behind their words lie deeds and sacrifices. The mightiness of their words grows with the distance, just as the force of attraction increases in a stone dropped from a high tower. Emigration is the first symptom of approaching upheaval.

Russians abroad have yet another task. It is really time to acquaint Europe with Russia. Europe does not know us, it knows our government, our façade—and nothing else. For this acquaintance circumstances are singularly favourable; haughty airs no longer suit Europe nor should she loftily wrap herself in the mantle of contemptuous ignorance. *Das vornehme Ignorieren* about Russia is out of date in Europe, now that she has experienced a bourgeois republic and the Cossacks from Algiers, now that from the Danube to the

Atlantic she has been through a state of siege, now that the prisons and the galleys are full of men persecuted for their beliefs . . . let her learn to know better a people whose youthful force she has tried in battle, in battle from which it emerged victorious; let us tell her about this mighty and still unfathomed people which in its unobtrusive way has managed to create a state of sixty millions, which has grown in such a vigorous, marvellous fashion without losing the principle of community, and which was the first to maintain this principle through the initial upheavals of national development; about a people which has somehow miraculously contrived to preserve itself under the yoke of Mongol hordes and German bureaucrats, under the barrack-room discipline of the corporal's baton, and the degrading Tartar knout; which has retained the noble features, the lively mind and the generous sweep of a rich nature beneath the yoke of serfdom, and which, in answer to the Tsar's order to educate itself, replied a hundred years later with the prodigious phenomenon of Pushkin. Let the Europeans get to know their neighbour: they only fear him, but they should know what it is that they fear.

Until now we have been unpardonably modest and too conscious of our oppressive lack of rights, and have forgotten all that is good, full of hope and promise in our national life. We had to wait for a German[1] to recommend us to Europe! For shame! Will I succeed in achieving something? I do not know. I hope so.

And so farewell my friends for a long while. . . . Give me your hands, your support. For I need both. After that . . . who knows? What have we not seen of late! It may not be so *far away* as it may seem, that day when we shall all meet in Moscow as of old and shall fearlessly raise our glasses to the toast: 'For Russia and sacred freedom'.

[1]A. von Haxthausen (1792–1866), a Rhineland baron who travelled in Russia in 1843 and later wrote a book on the Russian agrarian system.

My heart refuses to believe that that day will not come; it sinks at the thought of a parting for ever. Shall I really never see again those streets along which I used to walk so often, full of youthful dreams; those houses, so wrapped in memories; our Russian villages, our peasants, whom I used to think about with love in the very South of Italy? . . . It cannot be! . . . And yet, if it is—then I bequeath my toast to my children, and dying on alien soil, I shall preserve my faith in the future of the Russian people and bless it from the distant land of my voluntary exile.

I

BEFORE THE STORM[1]

(A Conversation on deck)

Ist's denn so grosses Geheimnis was Gott und der Mensch und die Welt sei?
Nein, doch niemand hoert's gerne, da bleibt es geheim.
GOETHE

'. . . I agree that there is a great deal of force, truth, boldness, and, indeed, even humour in your view, but I cannot accept it—it may be a matter of one's constitution, of one's nervous system. . . . You will not have any disciples till you discover how to change the blood in our veins.'

'Perhaps you are beginning to incline towards my point of view for you are looking for physiological causes, you are turning to nature.'

'Yes, but not in order to find rest or relief from suffering, nor to look down upon this troubled world from some remote Olympian height with the dispassionate detachment of a Goethe, nor to enjoy the spectacle of this seething chaos in its impotent efforts to find form and stability.'

'You are being distinctly disagreeable, but your words don't touch me; if I tried to grasp the meaning of life, it was with no ulterior purpose; I wanted to discover something, to penetrate a little further; what I had heard and read did not satisfy me, didn't provide an explanation; on the contrary, it led to contradictions or absurdities. I wasn't seeking either comfort or despair, and that because I was

[1]Dialogue written in 1847, apparently based on conversations with a former member of Herzen's Moscow circle, I. Galakhov.

young. Now I prize every fleeting pleasure, every minute of joy, for there are fewer and fewer of them. Then I looked only for the truth in order to understand as much as I could; whether I found much or understood much—I do not know. I should not say that my present point of view is a particularly consoling one, but I have grown calmer: I have stopped being angry with life because it does not give what it cannot give—that is all I have managed to achieve.'

'As for me, I do not want to stop being angry or suffering; this is so much a human right that I should not dream of surrendering it; my indignation is my protest; I do not want to make peace.'

'Anyhow, there is no one to make peace with. You say that you do not want to cease suffering. You mean that you do not want to accept the truth as it is revealed to you by your own thought—perhaps it would not demand suffering from you. You repudiate all logic in advance—you give yourself the right to accept or reject consequences as you choose. Remember the Englishman who all his life never recognized Napoleon as Emperor; which did not prevent Napoleon from being crowned twice. So stubborn a desire to remain at odds with the world is not only inconsistent, it is the height of vanity; human beings like a dramatic effect, to play a part, especially a tragic one; to suffer is good, noble, suggests misfortune. And that is by no means all. This attitude is not merely vanity—it is immense cowardice. Do not be offended by these words; fear of discovering the truth makes many prefer suffering to analysis. Pain distracts, absorbs, comforts . . . yes, yes, it comforts, and above all, like every occupation, it prevents men from looking into themselves, into life. Pascal said that people play cards in order not to be alone with themselves; we are constantly looking for this card or that—we are even willing to lose, if only we can forget reality. Our life is a constant flight from ourselves, as though we were pursued and frightened by the pangs of conscience. As soon as man stands on his own feet, he starts to shout, so as not to hear the voices that resound within; when he is sad, he runs in search of entertainment; when he has nothing to do, he invents tasks for himself; in his hatred of solitude he makes friends with everyone, reads everything, takes an interest in the affairs of others, and gets married in no time. This is the haven—family life and family quarrels will leave little room for thought. It is not, somehow, proper for a family man to think much—he should not have so much time on his hands. Those who do not make a success even of this kind of life simply go and get drunk on goodness knows what—wine, numismatics, cards, races, women, making money, good works—or plunge into mysticism, or become Jesuits, and lay upon themselves monstrous labours, which still seem lighter to them than a kind of ominous truth that slumbers within them. In this fear of all inquiry, fear lest the absurdity of the subject of inquiry be glimpsed, in these invented preoccupations, these unreal misfortunes, cluttering up our every step with artificial complexities, we move through life half-asleep, and die in a fever of nonsense and triviality. Strange thing: in all that does not concern the problems of inner life people are intelligent, audacious, penetrating; they consider themselves, for instance, as situated outside nature and study her conscientiously; here, however, we find a different method, other tactics. Is it not sad to be so frightened of the truth, of inquiry? Granted that many dreams will fade, that things will not be easier—but more difficult; still it is morally better, worthier, more manly, not to be childish. If people looked at one another as they look at nature, they would laugh and come down from their pedestals and senatorial chairs, they would look at life more simply, and stop being beside themselves with anger because life does not obey their haughty commands, their private whims. You, for instance, expected from life something quite different from what it gave you; instead of appreciating what it has given, you are angry with it. This indignation is perhaps a good thing—a sharp ferment that spurs man to action and movement, but, after all, that is merely the initial impulse; one cannot remain merely indignant and spend one's life lamenting one's failures, in a constant state of struggle and resentment! Tell me frankly: how did you convince yourself that your demands were real?'

'I did not invent them; they were born naturally within me; the more I thought about them afterwards, the more clearly I perceived their wisdom, their justice—these are my proofs. This is neither perversion nor aberration. Thousands of others, our whole generation, suffer in almost the same way, to a greater or less extent, according to circumstances and their degree of development—the higher the degree of development the greater the suffering. Universal grief is the supreme characteristic of our times. A dull weight oppresses the soul of contemporary man; the consciousness of his moral helplessness torments him; the absence of belief in anything whatever causes him to grow old before his time. I regard you as an exception; besides, your detachment seems to me suspect. It is too like dead despair, the detachment of a man who has lost, not only hope, but also lack of hope. It is an unnatural calm. Nature, true in all she does, as you yourself have said on several occasions, must be genuine also in this manifestation of grief, of despondency. The universality of it gives it certain rights. You must admit this; it is surely your—precisely your—point of view that makes it difficult to argue against it.'

'Why argue? I ask for nothing better than to agree with you. The state of despondency of which you speak is indeed manifest, and has, of course, a right to be justified historically and, still more, to let a way of escape be found. Suffering, pain—is a challenge to battle; it is the warning cry of life, calling attention to danger. The world in which we live is dying—that is, the forms in which life manifests itself; no medicine will have any more effect on its decayed body. In order that the heirs may breathe freely, the body should be interred, but people insist on trying to cure it and delay its death. You must have known the numbing sadness, the lingering nervous uncertainty that pervades a house where someone is dying. Despair is fortified by hope, everyone's nerves are taut, the sound grow sick, things are at a standstill. The death of the sick man lifts the burden from the souls of those who remain. Tears flow, but the deadly period of waiting is over, and the disaster faces you in all its magnitude, irreparable, cutting off all hope; and then life begins to heal, to bring peace, to take a new turn. We are living at a time of great and painful agony—this is explanation enough of our despondency. Moreover, all earlier centuries have fostered in us sadness and morbid longings. Three hundred years ago, all that was simple, healthy, vital, was still crushed; thought hardly dared raise its voice; its position was like that of the Jews in the Middle Ages, cunning from sheer necessity, slavish, perpetually alert to danger. Our mind was formed under these influences; it grew and matured in this unhealthy atmosphere; from Catholic mysticism it turned naturally to idealism, retaining fear of everything natural, the remorse of a betrayed conscience, demands for some unattainable bliss. It remained in conflict with life, and in a state of unhappy romantic yearning, it inured itself to suffering and disintegration. How long ago was it that, terrified from childhood, we ceased to kill in ourselves the most innocent desires? How long ago did we cease to shudder when finding in our soul passionate impulses unrecorded in the tariff of romanticism? You were saying just now that the demands that distress us developed naturally. That is both true and untrue—everything is natural; scrofula comes from bad food and a bad climate quite naturally, nevertheless we consider it something alien to the organism. Education does to us what Hannibal's father did to his son.

It extorts from us a vow before we reach full consciousness, it entangles us in a moral bondage which we regard as necessary through false delicacy, through the difficulty of ridding ourselves of something injected into us so early, ultimately through our laziness in understanding what it is all about. Education deceives us before we are in a condition to understand, it convinces children of the impossible, and it cuts them off from any free and direct relationship to the object. As we grow up we realize that nothing fits, neither thought nor ways of life, that what we were taught to lean upon is fragile and rotten, that what we were warned against as poisonous is beneficial; crushed and bewildered, taught to obey authority and rules, finally, with the years, we emerge into freedom, each gropes his way towards the truth, struggling and blundering. Thirsty for knowledge, we listen at keyholes, we try to peer through chinks: cheating, pretending, we consider truth a vice, and contempt for lies impudence. Is it so strange that after this we are unable to organize either the inner or the outer life, that we demand too much, sacrifice too much, scorn the possible, are indignant because what is impossible scorns us. We rebel against the natural conditions of life, and submit to every kind of arbitrary nonsense. All our civilization is like that, it has developed in the midst of internecine moral strife; breaking out from the schools and monasteries, it did not emerge into life, but sauntered through it, like Faust, merely to take a look at it, to reflect upon it, and then to withdraw from the rude mob into *salons*, academies and books. It has made the whole journey under two banners: "Romanticism for the heart" was inscribed on one, "Idealism for the mind" on the other. That is where the greater part of the disorder of our lives comes from. We do not like the simple, we do not respect nature as we ought, we want to order her about, we want to cure her by magic spells, and are then surprised that the patient is no better; medicine offends us by its independence and self-sufficiency;

we want alchemy, magic, but life and nature go their ways indifferent, submitting to man only to the extent to which he has learnt to work by their very methods.'

'You seem to take me for a German poet, and one moreover of a past generation, the sort who revolted against having a body, against having to eat, and looked for ethereal maidens, "another nature, another sun". I want neither magic nor mystery, only to escape from that state of mind which you have described ten times more acutely than I; to escape from moral impotence, from opinions pitifully divorced from practice, from the chaos in which we ultimately cease to distinguish friend from foe; I am disgusted to see, wherever I turn, only torturers or tortured. What magic does one need to convince people that they have only themselves to blame for the wretched way they live; to make it clear to them, for instance, that one must not rob a beggar; that it is disgusting to indulge in rich meals before a man dying of hunger; that murder is equally horrible whether done by stealth at night on a highway, or openly by the light of day in the public square to the roll of drums; that it is contemptible to say one thing and do another . . . in a word, all those new truths that have been said, repeated, printed from the days of the Seven Sages—and must, I think, have been pretty old even then. Moralists and priests thunder forth from pulpits, preach morality, denounce sins, read the Gospel, expound Rousseau—no one contradicts what they say and no one acts on it.'

'To tell you the truth—all this is not worth worrying about. All these lessons and sermons are mostly wrong, impracticable, and more confusing than the simple facts of ordinary everyday life. The trouble is that thought always runs far ahead; men cannot keep pace with their teachers. Take our own age: a few individuals almost brought about a revolution the results of which neither they themselves nor the people were able to consolidate. The more progressive thought that they had only to say: "Take up thy bed and walk", and everything would start moving. They were mistaken. The people knew them as little as they knew the people, and did not believe them. Without noticing that there was no one behind them, these men led on and marched forward. Then, suddenly realizing what had happened, they began to shout to the laggards—to wave, to call to them, to shower abuse on them; but too late; the others were too far behind. Their voices did not carry, and besides their language was not one familiar to the masses. We find it painful to admit that we live in a world that has outlived its emotions and its senses, that it is senile, exhausted, that it obviously has not enough strength or character to rise to the height of its own ideas. We are sorry for the old world. We have grown used to it as to our own home. In the very effort of destroying it, we support it, we try to adjust our own convictions to its unwieldy mass, and will not see that the first sign of them spells its death sentence. We wear clothes made to fit not us but our grandparents. Our brain has been formed under the influence of past conditions. There is much that it cannot grasp, or sees from the wrong angle. People have arrived at their present state with so much effort, it seems to them such a blessed haven after the madness of feudalism and the stupefying oppression that followed it, that they are afraid to change it; they have become frozen in its forms, they are used to them; habit has replaced affection, the horizon has narrowed, all generosity of mind has ebbed, the will is weak.'

'What a wonderful picture. You should add that, alongside these contented creatures whom the present regime fits like a glove, there are on the one hand, the poor, undeveloped common people, savage, backward, hungry, in a hopeless struggle against want, destroyed by drudgery which cannot support them; on the other hand, we ourselves, we who have recklessly run ahead, the surveyors planting the stakes of a new world of which we shall never even see the rising of the foundations. Of all the hopes, of all the life that has slipped through our fingers (and how it has!) if there's anything left, it is faith in the future; sometime, long after our death, the house for which we have cleared the site will be built and it will be comfortable and pleasant—for others.'

'Though of course there is no reason to believe that the new world will be built according to our plans. . . .'

. . . The young man gave a discontented toss of the head, and for a moment glanced at the sea—the total calm continued, a heavy cloud imperceptibly moved over their heads. It was so low that the smoke of the ship, settling in the air, mingled with it; the sea was black, there was no freshness in the air. . . .

'You are doing to me,' he said, after a silence, 'what robbers do to travellers; having stripped me completely you are still not satisfied; you are after the last tatters which keep the cold from me, after the hair on my skin. You have forced me to doubt a great deal, but the future still remained for me; now you are taking that away, stealing my hopes, murdering my dreams, like Macbeth.'

'I thought I was more like a surgeon, who cuts away dead flesh.'

'Yes, you are right. I think that is even better. The surgeon cuts away the sick part of the body without replacing it with a healthy part.'

'And in the process saves a life, liberating it from the heavy chains of a chronic illness.'

'We know your kind of liberation. You open the prison doors and want to drive the convict out into the open, assuring him that he is free. You demolish the Bastille, but build nothing in its place, leaving only an empty site.'

'It would be wonderful if things were as you say, but, alas, the ruins and the rubble are everywhere in the way.'

'In the way of what? What is this mission of ours, where is our banner? What *do* we, and what do we not, believe in?'

'We believe in everything, but we do not believe in

ourselves. You are looking for a banner, I am trying to lose one. You want a book of rules, while I think that when one reaches a certain age one ought to be ashamed of having to use one. You have just said that we are putting up signposts to the new world. . . .'

'And then they are torn up from their foundations by the spirit of negation and analysis. Your view of life is much gloomier than mine, and your words of comfort are designed to give an even more terrible description of our present plight. If even the future is not ours, then our whole civilization is a lie—the dream of a girl of fifteen, which she will smile at when she is twenty-five; our labours are absurd, our efforts ludicrous, our hopes those of a Danubian peasant. But perhaps this is what you want to say: that we should abandon our civilization, give it up, and take our place once more among the backward peoples.'

'No, one cannot give up progress. How can one not know what one does know? Our civilization is the finest flower of modern life. And who could want to sacrifice his chances of development? But what has this to do with the realization of our ideals? Where are the necessities in virtue of which the future must act the precise role that we have devised for it?'

'Oh, so according to you, our ideas have led us to unrealizable hopes, absurd expectations; together with them—the last fruits of our efforts—we are caught by the waves sweeping over a sinking ship. The future is not ours: we have nothing to do with the present; we have no means of escape. For we are tied to this ship in life and in death. All that is left is to wait with folded hands for the waters to flood over us; anyone who is bored, or is braver than the rest, may jump into the sea.

> . . . Le monde fait naufrage
> Vieux bâtiment, usé par tous les flots,
> Il s'engloutit—sauvons-nous à la nage![1]

[1]Lines by Béranger on the death of Victor d'Escus and Auguste Lebras, two Romantic poets, who committed suicide in 1832 after the failure of their play.

'I ask for nothing better, but there is a difference between swimming to save oneself and drowning. The fate of the young men whom this song recalls is horrible; doubly martyrs, martyrs without faith, let their death lie heavy on the terrible society in which they lived. Let it be branded upon it, stamped on it for ever. But who on earth told you there is no other way out, no other escape, from this world of senility and agony—save death? You insult life. Abandon a world to which you do not belong if you really feel that it is alien to you. It cannot be saved, but save yourself from the danger of the falling ruins; in saving yourself you will save the future. What have you in common with that world? Its civilization? But by now that civilization belongs to you, not to it. It did indeed generate it—or, to be more correct, within it a civilization was generated; it is not even guilty of comprehending this civilization; its way of life is hateful to you and, indeed, it is not easy to like such an absurdity. Your sufferings? The world has not an inkling of them; and it knows nothing of your joys. You are young, it is old. See how haggard it looks, in its shabby livery; particularly since the 1830s, its face has acquired a dull, grey, muddy hue. This is the *facies hippocratica*, by which doctors tell that Death has lifted its scythe. It strives impotently to cling to life, to recapture it, to shake itself free of the disease, to taste pleasure, but it fails and falls back into a heavy, feverish slumber. All round it people are talking of *phalanstères*, of democracy, of socialism; it listens but doesn't understand a word, sometimes it smiles at this talk, and nods its head and remembers the dreams that it too once believed in before it grew to reason but hasn't believed in for many years now. . . . That is why it looks on with an old man's indifferent eye at communists and Jesuits, parsons and Jacobins, the brothers Rothschild and starving men alike; it looks on at all this as it rushes past, clutching in its fist a few francs, for the sake of which it is ready to die or murder. Leave the old man to end his days as best he can, in an almshouse. You can do nothing for him.'

'That's not so easy—quite apart from being repulsive. And where would one run away to? Where is this new Pennsylvania, ready for . . .'

'For old buildings out of new bricks? William Penn took an old world with him to a new soil; North America is merely a corrected edition of an old text—nothing more: whereas the Christians in Rome were Romans no longer; that kind of internal emigration is more effective.'

'The idea of retreating into oneself, severing the umbilical cord which binds us to our country, to the present, has been preached for years now, but doesn't seem particularly practicable. It appeals to people after every failure, after every loss of faith; mystics and freemasons, philosophers and *illuminati* have turned to it for refuge. They all pointed to the path of inner escape, but no one took it. Rousseau?—he, too, kept turning away from the world; he loved it passionately, and tore himself away from it because he couldn't live without it. His disciples continued to live his life, within the Convention, fought, suffered, killed others, left their heads on the scaffold, but never once left France, never left the boiling maelstrom of activity.'

'Their age was altogether unlike ours. An infinity of hope stretched before them. Rousseau and his disciples imagined that if their ideas of fraternity weren't realized, this must be because of material obstacles—here speech was repressed, there action curtailed—and with great consistency they marched boldly against everything that stood in the way of their ideas; it was a terrifying, a gigantic task, but they triumphed. Having triumphed, they thought: here we are at last. And there they were, indeed—on the guillotine; and that was the very best that could have happened to them; they died in the fullness of their faith, they were swept away by a vast wave, in the fury of the battle, in the full intoxicating joy of the struggle. They were so sure that, when peace returned, their ideal would be realized—without them, but realized it would be. Well, at least peace did return. How fortunate it was that all these enthusiasts were long in their graves! They would have had to realize that their cause hadn't advanced an inch, that their ideals remained ideals, that it is not enough to demolish the Bastille stone by stone to make free men out of convicts. You compare us to them, quite forgetting that we know the events of the fifty years since their death, that we have seen all the hopes of the theorists derided, and the demonic pattern of history makes a mock of their learning, their thought, their theories, turns the republic into a Napoleon, the revolution of 1830 into a deal on the Bourse. Having seen so much, we cannot share the hopes of our predecessors. Having studied revolutionary questions more profoundly, our demands are larger and wider than theirs, while theirs have remained as impractical as ever. On one side you have the logical consistency of thought, its successes; on the other its complete impotence before a world deaf, mute, powerless to grasp the idea of salvation in the form in which it is expressed—either because it is expressed badly or because its significance is purely theoretical, bookish, like for instance Roman philosophy, which never moved outside a small circle of educated men.'

'But then, which is right in your opinion? Theoretical thought, whose development and historical formation are in no way peculiar save for being conscious—or the fact of the contemporary world, which rejects thought and yet, like it, is the inevitable result of the past?'

'Both are completely right. All this confusion arises from the fact that life has its own embryogenesis which does not coincide with the dialectic of pure reason. I spoke just now of the ancient world—well, that's an example for you: instead of realizing the Republic of Plato or the Politics of Aristotle, it created the Roman Republic and the politics of their conquerors; instead of the utopias of Cicero and Seneca, the fiefs of the Lombards and German Law.'

'And are you predicting that our civilization will suffer the same fate as that of Rome? A comforting thought and a beautiful prospect.'

'Neither a beautiful nor an ugly one. What is it that surprises you in the notion—the tritest of all platitudes—that everything in the world is transient? Moreover civilizations do not perish as long as the human race continues to live without a complete break, for mankind has a good memory. Is Roman civilization not alive for us? And it has stretched far beyond the frontiers of surrounding life, just as ours has done; that is exactly why, on the one hand, it flowered so luxuriantly, so magnificently, and, on the other, it could not be realized in practice. It has brought much that was its own to the modern world, it gives us much, but the immediate future of Rome lay elsewhere—in catacombs, where persecuted Christians were hidden, in forests where bands of wild Germans wandered.'

'How is it that while everything in Nature is so purposive, civilization, its highest effort, the crown of the age, emerges from it as if by accident, drops out of life and finally fades away, leaving behind only a dim memory? Meanwhile mankind moves backward, leaves the high road, and then again begins to strain upwards, to end once more in the same gorgeous flower—magnificent, but without seed. . . . In your philosophy of history there is something that revolts the soul. Why all these efforts? The life of peoples becomes mere idle play, it piles grain on grain, pebble on pebble, until once again everything comes tumbling down to earth and men begin to crawl out from under the ruins, to clear a space and build huts for themselves out of moss, boards and fallen capitals, only to achieve, after centuries of long effort, destruction once more. It was not for nothing that Shakespeare said that history was a tale told by an idiot, signifying nothing.'

'That is just your melancholy view of things. You are like those monks who have nothing better to say to each other when they meet than a gloomy *memento mori*, or like those excessively sentimental souls who cannot recall that "man is born but to die" without shedding a tear. To look at the end and not at the action itself is the greatest of errors. Of what use to the plant is its bright, gorgeous flower, its intoxicating scent which will pass away? None at all. But nature is not so miserly, and does not disdain what is transient, what lives only in the moment. At every point she attains all that she can attain, she achieves the impossible—fragrance, delight, an idea . . . she goes on until she reaches the frontiers of development, reaches death itself, which cools her ardour, checks her poetic fantasy, her unbridled creative passion. Who will blame nature because flowers that bloom in the morning fade in the evening, because she has not bestowed on the rose or the lily the hardness of flint? And yet it is this mean and prosy attitude that we want to carry over into the world of history! Who has ventured to restrict civilization to the practical alone? What barrier does it know? It is boundless, like thought, like art; it traces the ideals of life, it dreams the apotheosis of its own being, but life is under no obligation to realize such fantasies and ideas, the more so since this would be only an improved edition of what was there before, and life loves novelty. Roman civilization was far higher, far more humane than the barbarian world, but in the very confusion of barbarism were the seeds of things not to be found in the civilization of Rome, and so barbarism triumphed despite the *Corpus Juris Civilis* and the wisdom of Roman philosophers. Nature rejoices in what has been attained, and reaches out beyond it; she has no desire to wrong what exists; let it live as long as it can, while the new is still growing. That is why it is so difficult to fit the work of nature into a straight line; nature hates regimentation, she casts herself in all directions and never marches forward in step. The German barbarians were, in their untutored spontaneity *potentialiter* higher than the civilized Romans.'

'I'm beginning to think that you're expecting a new barbarian invasion and migration of peoples.'

'I don't like prophesying. The future does not exist; it is created by the combination of a thousand causes, some necessary, some accidental, plus human will, which adds unexpected dramatic *dénouements* and *coups de théâtre*. History improvises, she rarely repeats herself . . . she uses every chance, every coincidence, she knocks simultaneously at a thousand gates . . . Who knows which may open?'

'Perhaps the Baltic gates, and then Russia will pour into Europe?'

'Perhaps.'

'Here we are, after all our philosophising, like a squirrel in a wheel, back to the *corsi e ricorsi* of old Vico.[1] We have returned to Rhea, perpetually bearing children in terrible pain for Saturn's supper. Only Rhea has now grown conscientious and no longer tries to slip in stones in place of the new-born; besides, it would not be worth the effort, for there is no Jupiter or Mars amongst them. . . . What is the purpose of all this? You move round and round the question, without solving it. Should children be born only to make a meal for their father? All in all, is the game worth the candle?'

'Of course it is! Especially as it isn't you who pay for it. You're dismayed because not all games are played to the end, but if they were they would be intolerably tedious. Long, long ago, Goethe used to tell us that beauty is transient because only the transient can be beautiful; this offends people. Man has an instinctive desire to preserve all that delights him; he is born, *ergo* he wants to live for ever; he falls in love, he wants to love and be loved all his life as

[1] Giambattista Vico (1668–1744), Italian historian, jurist and philosopher, author of the *Scienza Nuova*; expounded a theory of recurrent historical cycles.

in the first moment of avowal. He is angry with life when he notices that at fifty his feelings haven't the freshness or sharpness they had at twenty. But such a stagnant immobility is repugnant to the spirit of life; life cares nothing for the survival of anything personal, individual; she always pours the whole of herself into the present moment, and while endowing people with a capacity for the fullest possible pleasure, insures neither existence nor pleasure, and accepts no responsibility for their continuance. In this ceaseless movement of all living things, in this universal change, nature renews herself and lives on; in them she is eternally young. That is why each historical moment is complete and self-contained, like each year with its spring and summer, its winter and autumn, its storms and fine weather. That is why each period is new, fresh, full of its own hopes, carrying within itself its own joys and sorrows. The present belongs to it. But human beings are not satisfied with this. They want the future to be theirs as well.'

'It is painful for man that he cannot see even in the future the harbour towards which he is moving. With melancholy anxiety, he contemplates the infinite road ahead of him and sees that he is just as far from his end after all efforts as he was a thousand, two thousand years ago!'

'And what, pray, is the end of the song that the singer sings? . . . The sounds that burst from her throat, the melody that dies as soon as it has resounded? If you look beyond your pleasure in them for something else, for some other end, you will find that the singer has stopped singing, and then you will have only memories, and regrets, and remorse because, instead of listening, you were waiting for something else. You are misled by categories not fitted to catch the flow of life. Think carefully: is this end that you seek—a programme, an order? Who conceived it, who declared it? Is it something inevitable or not? If it is, are we mere puppets? . . . Are we morally free beings, or wheels in a machine? I prefer to think of life, and therefore of history, as an end attained than as a means to something else.'

'You mean, in short, that the end of nature and history is just—you and me? . . .'

'Partly; plus the present state of everything existing. Everything is included in this: the legacy of past efforts and the seeds of all that is to come; the inspiration of the artist, the energy of the citizen, and the rapture of the youth who, at this very moment, somewhere or other, is stealing his way towards some secret arbour where his shy love awaits him—giving herself completely to the present, with no thought of the future or of an aim . . . and the joy of a fish splashing—there—in the moonlight . . . and the harmony of the entire solar system . . . in short, I could add "and so forth . . . and so forth . . . and so forth . . ." three times—as after some feudal title.'

'You are quite right when you speak of nature, but it seems to me that you have forgotten that throughout all the changes and confusions of history there runs a single red thread binding it into one aim. This thread—is progress, or perhaps you do not acknowledge progress?'

'Progress is the inalienable quality of uninterrupted conscious development: it consists in a retentive memory and the physiological perfection of man through social life.'

'Is it possible that in all this you do not see a goal?'

'Quite the opposite, I see here only a consequence. If progress is the end, for whom are we working? Who is this Moloch who, as the toilers approach him, instead of rewarding them, only recedes, and as a consolation to the exhausted, doomed multitudes crying "morituri te salutant", can give back only the mocking answer that after their death all will be beautiful on earth. Do you truly wish to condemn all human beings alive to-day to the sad role of caryatids supporting a floor for others some day to dance on . . . or of wretched galley slaves, up to their knees in mud, dragging a barge filled with some mysterious treasure and with the humble words "progress in the future" inscribed on its bows? Those who are exhausted fall in their tracks; others, with fresh forces take up the ropes; but there remains, as you said yourself, as much ahead as there was at the beginning, because progress is infinite. This alone should serve as a warning to people: an end that is infinitely remote is not an end, but, if you like, a trap; an end must be nearer—it ought to be, at the very least, the labourer's wage, or pleasure in the work done. Each age, each generation, each life had and has its own fullness; *en route*, new demands arise, new experiences, new methods; some capacities improve at the expense of others; finally, the cerebral tissue improves. . . . Why do you smile? . . . Yes, yes, indeed, the substance of the brain improves. How everything that is natural surprises and disconcerts you idealists, as once upon a time knights were astonished that the villeins could be seeking human rights! When Goethe was in Italy, he compared the skull of an ancient bull with that of one of our bulls, and found that the bones of our bull were finer and the pans of the large lobes of the brain broader; the ancient bull was obviously stronger than ours, but ours in his meek submission to man had developed further so far as the brain was concerned. Why do you consider man less capable of development than a bull? This generic growth is not an aim, as you suppose, but the hereditary characteristic of a succession of generations. The aim of each generation—is itself. Nature not only never makes one generation the means for the attainment of some future end, she does not concern herself with the future at all. Like Cleopatra, she is ready to dissolve a pearl in wine, for a moment's pleasure. Nature has the heart of a bacchante, of a *bayadère*.'

'And the poor lady is unable to realize her vocation! . . . A bacchante on a diet, a *bayadère* in mourning! . . . In our age, I must say, she seems really rather more like a repentant

Magdalen. Or has the brain, perhaps, taken a wrong turning?'

'Instead of jeering, you have said something much more sensible than you think. Any one-sided development always leads to the stunting of the other neglected parts. Children who are over-developed psychologically do not grow up normally, are physically feeble; through centuries of unnatural existence we have turned ourselves into idealists—we have created a form of artificial life, we have disturbed the equilibrium. We used to be great and strong, even happy in our detachment, in the bliss of our theories, but now we have gone beyond this stage and it has become intolerable to us. Meanwhile, the break with practical life has become terrifying; no one is to blame for that, either on one side or the other. Nature strained every muscle to overcome the limitations of the beast in man—but he has so over-stepped them that with one leg he is quite outside nature; this he has done because he is free. We talk so much about free will; we are so proud of it and, at the same time, annoyed that nobody leads us by the hand and that we stumble and must take the consequences of our actions. I am ready to repeat your words that the brain has grown one-sidedly because of idealism; people have begun to notice this and are now moving in another direction. They will be cured of idealism as they have been of other historical diseases—chivalry, Catholicism, Protestantism. . . .'

'But you must agree that the path of development through deviation and disease is a very strange one.'

'Yes, but the path is not determined. . . . Nature has hinted only vaguely, in the most general terms, at her intentions, and has left all the details to the will of man, circumstances, climate, and a thousand conflicts. The struggle, the reciprocal action of natural forces and the forces of will, the consequences of which one cannot know in advance, give an overwhelming interest to every historical epoch. If humanity marched straight towards some kind of result, then there would be no history, only logic; humanity would have come to rest, a finished article, in an absolute *status quo*, like animals. But all this is fortunately impossible, unnecessary, and worse than the existing situation. The organism of the animal gradually develops an instinct; in man the development goes further. He develops *reason* and does so painfully, slowly: it exists neither in nature nor outside nature; one has to achieve it and come to terms with it as best one may, because there is no *libretto*. If there were a *libretto*, history would lose all interest, become unnecessary, boring, ludicrous; the grief of Tacitus and the joy of Columbus would turn into a game, into buffoonery; great men would be so many heroes strutting on a stage who, whether they acted well or badly, would inevitably move towards and reach a definite dénouement. In history, all is improvisation, all is will, all is *ex tempore*; there are no frontiers, no itineraries. There exist conditions, sacred discontent; the flame of life and the eternal challenge to the fighters to try their strength, to go where they will, where there is a road; and where there is none, genius will blast a path.'

But suppose, unluckily, no Columbus emerged?'

'Cortez will do it for him. Geniuses are almost always to be found when they are needed. Besides, there is no need for them. People will arrive eventually, they will arrive by another route—a more difficult one. Genius is the luxury of history, its poetry, its *coup d'état*, its flourish, the triumph of its creativeness.'

'All this is very well, but it seems to me that with such indecision, such licence, history might go on for ever or come to an end tomorrow.'

'No doubt. People will not die of boredom if the human race remains alive too long, though probably people will encounter some limit concealed in the very nature of man, some physiological conditions that one cannot surmount and remain human, but really there will be no lack of activity, of occupation. Three-quarters of what we do is a repetition of what has been done by others. You can see from this that history could go on for millions of years. On the other hand, I have nothing against history ending tomorrow. Anything can happen! Encke's comet [1] hits the world, a geological cataclysm shakes the earth's surface and throws everything upside-down, gaseous fumes make breathing impossible for half an hour—and there you have history's finale.'

'Pouf, what horrors! You frighten me, as one frightens small children, but I assure you that none of this will happen. Would it have been worth while to have had a development for three thousand years with the pleasant final prospect of suffocating from sulphuric fumes? How can you not see that this is an absurdity?'

'I am surprised that you have not yet become used to the ways of life. In nature, as in the souls of men, there slumber countless forces and possibilities; under suitable conditions they develop—and develop furiously; they may fill the whole world, or they may fall by the wayside, take a new direction, stop, collapse. The death of one man is no less absurd than the end of the whole human race. Who guaranteed the immortality of a planet? It will be as little able to survive a revolution in the solar system as the genius of Socrates could the hemlock—possibly it will not be offered hemlock . . . possibly. . . . Now I'm back where I began. On the whole, Nature is perfectly indifferent to the result. She cannot be diminished, she will never lose anything, nothing can be taken from her, everything is in her however it changes. And she, having buried the human race, will lovingly begin all over again, with monstrous ferns and reptiles half a league long, probably with certain

[1] Johann Franz Encke (1791–1865) the director of the Berlin Observatory who discovered in 1819 the short period comet that goes by his name. At one time (in the 1830s) it was thought that it might collide with the Earth.

improvements suggested by new surroundings, new conditions.'

'Well, for human beings it is far from being a matter of indifference. I think that Alexander the Great would not be at all pleased to know that he has been used as glue, as Hamlet says.'

'About Alexander the Great I can reassure you—he will never know of it. Of course, it is not at all a matter of indifference to a man whether he is alive or not. From this one thing alone is clear; that one should make use of life, of the present; not in vain does Nature in all her utterances for ever beckon life onwards and whisper in every ear her *vivere memento*.'

'A waste of time! We are conscious of life through dull pain, through regrets which gnaw the heart, through the monotonous ticking of clocks. . . . It is hard to enjoy life to the full, to get drunk, knowing that the whole world is crumbling around you, and may well crush you. And that is not the worst—the worst is to die in old age, seeing that the ancient, tottering walls have no thought of crumbling. I know of no such suffocating period in history; there have been struggles, there has been suffering before now, but there was also some compensation; one could at least die with faith. We have nothing to die for and nothing to live for. . . . Just the time for enjoying life to the full!'

'And do you think that it was easier to live in decadent Rome?'

'Of course. Its fall was just as obvious as the world coming to replace it.'

'Obvious to whom? Do you really think that the Romans saw their age as we see it? Gibbon could never free himself from the fascination that ancient Rome exercises over every strong spirit. Remember how many centuries its agony lasted; for us that time is foreshortened because it is poor in events, poor in characters, because of the dreary monotony. It is just such periods, dumb, grey, that are particularly frightening for the people who live through them. After all, the year had the same three hundred and sixty-five days, then as now there were people with ardent spirits who withered away, lost in the crash of crumbling walls. What sounds of grief must have been torn from the human breast; even now the groans terrify the soul!'

'They could have had themselves baptized. . . .'

'The position of Christians was also very pitiful; for four centuries they remained hidden in catacombs, success seemed impossible, there were martyrs everywhere.'

'But they were upheld by fanatical faith—and it was justified.'

'Yet on the morrow of victory heresy showed itself; the pagan world broke into the sacred stillness of their brotherhood, and the Christian turned back with tears to the times of persecution and blessed their memory as he read the Martyrology.'

'You seem to be starting to console me by showing me that things have always been as bad as they are now.'

'No, I merely wanted to remind you that our age has not the monopoly of suffering and that you hold too cheap the afflictions of the past. Even before now thought was impatient enough, it wants everything at once, it loathes waiting—but life is not satisfied with abstract ideas, does not hurry, takes each step slowly because its steps are difficult to correct. Therein lies the tragic position of thinkers. . . . But, not to digress again, let me ask you now why you think that our world is so solid and long-lived? . . .'

For a long time large drops of rain had been falling upon us. The hollow rumble of thunder came closer, the flashes of lightning became brighter. Now the rain fell in torrents. Everyone rushed back to his cabin; the ship creaked and the tossing became unbearable—the conversation did not go on.

ROME, VIA DEL CORSO
December 31st, 1847

II

AFTER THE STORM

TOGETHER we have lived through those painful, ghastly, degrading June days. I offer you the first tears to burst from my heart now that they are over. Yes, tears . . . I am not ashamed of them. Do you remember the Marseillaise of Rachel?[1] Only now can we appreciate it to the full. All Paris sang the Marseillaise—the blind beggars and Grisi,[2] the street urchins and the soldiers. The Marseillaise, as one journalist put it, became the *pater noster* after February 24th. Only now has it died down, for its strains can scarcely thrive in a state of siege. The Marseillaise, after February 24th was a cry of joy, victory, power, menace; the cry of might and triumph. . . . And then Rachel sang the Marseillaise. Her song frightened me and I wept and came away broken. Do you remember? It was the knell of death tolling at the wedding feast, it was a reproach, a dread premonition, a moan of despair amidst hope. . . . The Marseillaise of Rachel called men to a feast of blood and revenge. Where flowers had been scattered, there she strewed juniper. Good Frenchmen said: This is not the bright Marseillaise of 1848, but a sombre one, that of the days of the Terror. They were mistaken. In '93 there was no such song, such a song could have sprung from an artist's heart only after the betrayal of February 24th, only before the crime of the June days.

[1]Elisa Félix (1820–58). Known as Rachel. The most famous actress of her day who contributed greatly to the revived interest in classical tragedy.

[2]Giulia Grisi (1811–69). Celebrated Italian coloratura soprano.

Do you remember how this woman made her appearance —pensive, wearing a plain white blouse, leaning her head on her hands; she moved slowly, with a sombre air and began to sing, in an undertone. . . . The agonizing sorrow of that sound came close to despair. She was calling men to battle, but she had no faith that they would go. . . . This was a plea, this was remorse. . . . Then suddenly, out of that weak chest a cry bursts forth . . . a scream—full of fury and passion.

'Aux armes, citoyens,
Qu'un sang impur abreuve nos sillons'

she adds with the heartlessness of a hangman. Surprised herself by the ecstasy to which she has surrendered, she begins the second verse even more faintly, more despairingly; and once more calls men to battle, to blood. For a moment the woman in her gains the upper hand; she throws herself on her knees, and the bloody challenge becomes a prayer; love conquers, she cries and presses the banner to her heart. . . . *Amour sacré de la patrie*! But she is suddenly ashamed, she has leapt to her feet and darts away, waving the banner, with the cry: *Aux armes, citoyens*! The crowd did not dare bring her back.

The article that I am giving you is *my* Marseillaise. Farewell! Read these lines to my friends. Do not be unhappy. I dare not call you by name, nor name myself. In the place to which you are going, weeping is a crime and to listen to it is a sin.

PARIS, 1848
August 1st

Pereat!

Women weep in order to relieve their hearts. But we do not know how to weep. In the place of tears, I want to write;

not in order to describe or to explain the blood-stained events, but simply to talk about them, to give vent to words, tears, thoughts, gall. How can we at this moment describe, collect information, assess what has happened? Our ears are still ringing with the sound of shot, the clatter of galloping cavalry, and the heavy muffled sound of the gun carriages rattling through the dead streets; isolated moments still flicker in the mind's eye, a wounded man on a stretcher pressing his hand to his side and a few drops of blood running down it, omnibuses filled with corpses, prisoners with their hands bound, cannons on the Place de la Bastille, a camp at the Porte Saint-Denis and another on the Champs Élysées, and the grim nocturnal cry: *Sentinelle, prenez garde à vous*! How can one begin to describe now—the brain is too inflamed, the blood prickles.

To sit in one's rooms with hands folded, to have no possibility of leaving the house, to hear, all round one, from near and afar, shots and cannon fire and screams, the beat of drums, and to know that a few steps away blood is being shed, that people are stabbing and killing, that nearby they are dying—this is enough to kill one, to drive one insane. I did not die, but I have aged, and I am recovering from those June days as from a heavy sickness.

And how triumphantly they began! On the 23rd, at about four in the afternoon, before dinner, I was walking along the Seine towards the Hôtel de Ville; the shops were being shut, detachments of the National Guard, looking menacing, were marching in various directions, the sky was covered with cloud, it was raining. I stopped on the Pont-Neuf. . . . There was a sudden flash of lightning from behind a cloud, peals of thunder came one after another and in the middle of this the measured lingering sound of the tocsin rang out from the tower of St Sulpice. The proletariat, betrayed once again, was calling its brothers to arms. A few rays of sunlight gleaming brightly from underneath a cloud cast an unusual radiance over the cathedral and all the buildings along the river. One could hear the drums from all sides; the artillery was moving slowly from the Place du Carrousel.

I listened to the thunder and the tocsin and gazed avidly at this panorama of Paris; it was as though I was taking my leave of it. At that moment I loved Paris passionately. It was my last tribute to the great town; after the June days it grew hateful to me.

On the other side of the river barricades were being raised in all the streets and alleys. I can still see the gloomy faces of the men dragging stones; women and children were helping them. A young student from the Polytechnic climbed up on to an apparently completed barricade, planted the banner and started singing the Marseillaise in a soft, sad, solemn voice; all the workers joined in and the chorus of this great song, resounding from behind the stones of the barricades, gripped one's soul. . . . The tocsin was still tolling. Meanwhile, the artillery clattered across the bridge and General Bedeau [1] standing there raised his field-glasses to inspect the *enemy* positions. . . .

At that moment everything could still have been prevented—the republic saved—and with it the freedom of Europe; there was still time to make peace. . . . But the stupid and clumsy government did not know how to do this, the Assembly did not wish it; the reactionaries sought revenge, blood, retribution for February 24th; the storehouses of the *National* [2] provided them with men of action.

Well, what have you to say, my dear Prince Radetsky [3]

[1] Marie-Alphonse Bedeau (1804–63), French general of considerable experience in North Africa. Seriously wounded in the June days. Exiled after December 2nd.

[2] *Le National:* organ of bourgeois republican party, edited by Marrast.

[3] Johann Josef Wenzel, Count Radetsky (1766–1858), Austrian general who served against the Turks and Napoleon. Later commander-in-chief of Austrian troops in Italy, and responsible for suppression of revolution of 1848.

and Your Serene Highness, Count Paskevich-Erivansky?[1] You would not do as assistants to Cavaignac.[2] Metternich and all the members of the Third department of His Imperial Majesty's private Chancery are gentle children, *de bons enfants*, compared with a pack of growling shopkeepers.

On the evening of June 26th, after the victory of the *National* over Paris, we heard the sound of gunfire at short regular intervals. . . . We glanced at one another, our faces looked green. 'The firing squads' we all said with one voice, and turned away from each other. I pressed my forehead to the windowpane. Moments like these make one hate for a whole decade, seek revenge all one's life. *Woe to those who forgive such moments!*

After the slaughter which lasted four days, silence descended, the calm of a siege; the streets were still cordoned off and only very occasionally would you see a carriage. The arrogant National Guard, with an expression of savage, dull cruelty, protected its shops, threatening passers-by with butt and bayonet; the exultant crowds of the drunken Garde Mobile marched along the boulevards, singing: '*Mourir pour la patrie*'. Boys of sixteen, seventeen, boasted of the blood of their brothers which had dried on their hands; they were thrown flowers by shopgirls who ran out from behind their counters to greet the victors. Cavaignac carted about with him in his carriage some monster or other who had killed dozens of Frenchmen. The bourgeoisie was

[1]Count Ivan Fedorovich Paskevich (1782–1856). Russian general. Distinguished himself at Austerlitz. Fought against Persians and Turks: suppressed Polish rising of 1831 with great brutality: later viceroy of Poland. Led Russian army that helped Austria against Hungary in 1849.

[2]Louis-Eugène Cavaignac (1802–57), general of republican sympathies. Recalled to France in 1848, he was elected a Member of National Assembly and made Minister of War. In charge of suppression of June rising. Ran unsuccessfully as candidate for Presidency against Louis-Napoleon.

triumphant. And the houses in the Faubourg Saint-Antoine were still smoking; the walls broken by shells were falling in, the interiors of rooms laid bare gaped like stone wounds . . . broken furniture was lying in rotting heaps, pieces of broken mirrors glistened amongst the litter. But where are the owners, the tenants, where are they? No one gave them a thought. Here and there were men scattering sand in the streets, but the blood nevertheless kept oozing through. . . . No one was allowed near the Panthéon which had been riddled with shells; tents were pitched on the boulevards; horses were nibbling at the carefully tended trees in the Champs Élysées; hay, armour, saddles, were strewn across the Place de la Concorde. In the Tuileries soldiers cooked their soup by the railings. Paris had not seen this even in 1814.

A few days went by—and Paris began to resume its normal appearance. Crowds of idle strollers once again appeared on the boulevards, elegant ladies drove out in their carriages and cabriolets to inspect the ruins of the houses and the traces of the desperate battle. Only the frequent patrols and the gangs of prisoners were there to remind one of the dreadful days; only then did the past become clear. Somewhere in Byron there is a description of a night battle; the bloody details are concealed by the darkness and only at dawn when the battle has long been over can one see the remains, a dagger, a blood-stained garment. Such a dawn was now breaking in the soul, lighting up the terrible devastation. Half our hopes, half our convictions had been killed, ideas of negation and despair stirred in our mind and took root. We could hardly believe that after so many ordeals, after all the trials of modern scepticism, there was still so much left in our souls to destroy.

After such convulsions the human being cannot remain what he was. Either his soul becomes more religious, clinging with desperate stubbornness to its convictions and finds comfort in the very absence of hope, and the man flowers again, singed by the lightning, carrying death in his breast; or else gathering up all his strength he bravely surrenders his last hopes, grows soberer still and does not try to retain the last feeble leaves which the rude, autumn wind carries away.

Which is better? It is hard to tell.

One leads to the bliss of lunacy.

The other to the unhappiness of knowledge.

Choose for yourself. The one is very secure, because it takes everything away. The other offers no security, but gives you much. I choose knowledge, and, let it deprive me of the last consolation, I will wander as a moral pauper through the world, but the childish hopes, the youthful dreams must be torn out by the roots. Off with them to the bar of incorruptible reason!

Within every man there is a permanent revolutionary tribunal, there is a merciless Fouquier-Tinville and, above all, there is a guillotine. Sometimes the judge may nod, the guillotine grow rusty, and then all that is false, obsolete, romantic, weak raises its head, until suddenly some wild shock rouses the dormant court, the slumbering hangman. Then rough justice begins. The slightest concession, act of compassion, mercy, lead back to the past and leave the chains intact. There is no choice—one must either slaughter and go forward or pardon and falter half-way.

Who does not remember his romance with logic, who does not recollect how the first seed of doubt fell into his soul, does not remember the first bold moment of inquiry, and how it grew and grew until it reached the most sacred possessions of the soul? This is the terrible tribunal of reason. It is not as easy as it seems to condemn beliefs to death; it is hard to part with thoughts that we have grown up with, have got used to, thoughts that have comforted and consoled us; to sacrifice them seems ingratitude. Yes, but in the milieu of the tribunal there is no gratitude, sacrilege is not known there, and if revolution, like Saturn, devours its children, then denial, like Nero, kills its mother to rid itself of the past. Men are afraid of their own logic and having summoned the Church and the State, family and morality, good and evil, to face logic's judgment, they then try to save the remnants, the fragments of the past. Having repudiated Christianity, they cling to the immortality of the soul, to idealism, to Providence. People who have until then marched together here part ways: some go to the right, others to the left; some give up half-way and remain, like milestones, indicating how much has been accomplished: others drop the last burden of the past and boldly walk on. In passing from the old world to the new, you can take nothing with you.

Reason is, like the Convention, merciless, severe, no respecter of persons, it stops at nothing, it brings the Supreme Being itself into the dock. Good king Theology will duly have his January 21st.[1] This trial, like the trial of Louis XVI, is the touchstone for the Girondins; everything that is weak and half-hearted, runs away or lies, does not vote, or votes without conviction. And yet the people having passed sentence think that after executing the King there is nothing more to execute and that on January 22nd the republic is complete and happy. As if atheism were enough to abolish religion, as though it were enough to kill Louis XVI to abolish monarchy! There is an astonishing resemblance between the phenomenology of terror and that of logic. Terror began precisely after the execution of the King; after him there appeared on the scaffold the noble youths of the revolution, brilliant, eloquent—weak. One felt sorry for them, but it was impossible to save them, and their heads fell and were followed by Danton's leonine head, and that of the Revolu-

[1]Louis XVI was executed by order of the revolutionary tribunal on January 21st, 1793.

tion's spoilt darling, Camille Desmoulins.[1] But now, surely now, it is all over? No, now comes the turn of the incorruptible hangmen; they will be executed because they believed in the possibility of democracy in France, because they executed in the name of equality. Yes, executed like Anacharsis Cloots,[2] who dreamt of the brotherhood of peoples a few days before the Napoleonic era, a few years before the Congress of Vienna.

The world will not know liberty until everything religious and political is transformed into something simple, human, susceptible to criticism and denial. Logic, when it comes of age, detests canonized truths; it demotes them from angelic rank to human status, it converts holy mysteries into plain truths; it holds nothing sacrosanct and if the Republic arrogates to itself the same rights as the Monarchy, it will despise it as much as it did the Monarchy; nay, even more. Monarchy has no meaning; it is maintained by force, whereas the word 'republic' makes the heart beat faster. Monarchy is itself a religion; the republic has no mystical saving-clauses, no Divine Right, it stands on the same level with us all. It is not enough to despise the crown, one must give up respecting the Phrygian cap; it is not enough not to consider *lèse majesté* a crime, one must look on *salus populi* as being one.

It is time for man to put the republic on trial, along with

[1]Camille Desmoulins (1762–94). One of the most brilliant of the French revolutionaries, inspired by the ideal of the classical republic. Attached himself first to Mirabeau, and then to Danton. Protested against excesses of the Terror, and was executed along with Danton, March 30th, 1794.

[2]Jean Baptiste Cloots (1755–94). A German baron, who conceived the idea of a world state, with Paris as its capital. Assumed name of Anacharsis and travelled Europe preaching his doctrine. Supported the French revolution, elected a deputy after September massacres and voted for execution of the King. Denounced by Robespierre as an aristocrat and an atheist, and executed March 23rd, 1794.

its legislation, its system of representation, all our notions about the citizen and his relations to other citizens and to the State. There will be many executions: things nearest and dearest will have to be sacrificed—merely to sacrifice the detestable is not the problem. This is the whole point: to surrender what we love if we are convinced that it is not true. This is our real task. We have not been called to be the harvesters but to be the executioners of the past, to persecute it, to destroy it, to recognize it in all its guises and to offer it up to the future. If the past is triumphant in fact, let us kill it in the idea, in the conviction, in the name of human thought. There is no one to make concessions to: the tricolour of concessions is too stained—the June blood will take a long time to dry. And whom is it anyhow we are to spare? All the disintegrating elements reveal themselves in all their pathetic absurdity, in all their repulsive lunacy. What do you respect? A *popular* government—is that it? Whom are you sorry for? Paris perhaps.

For three months men elected by universal vote, the chosen deputies of the land of France, did nothing, and then they suddenly rose to their full height to show the world an unprecedented spectacle of eight hundred men behaving as one villain, as one monster. Blood flowed in torrents, and they could not find a single word of love or reconciliation; everything that was generous and human was drowned in cries of indignation and revenge; the voice of the dying Affre [1] could not touch the heart of this many-voiced Caligula, this Bourbon turned into small change. They pressed to their heart the National Guard, the killers of unarmed men. Senard showered blessings upon Cavaignac, and Cavaignac melted into pathetic tears, having fulfilled all the villainies pointed out to him by the representatives' accusing fingers. But the sinister minority lay low.

[1] Denis-Auguste Affre (1793–1848). Archbishop of Paris. Killed in the June Days while trying to persuade the soldiers to stop fighting.

The *Mountain* hid behind the clouds, pleased not to have been executed or left to rot in cellars; silently it looked on at the disarming of the citizens and the decrees of deportation, at the imprisonment of human beings for everything under the sun—for not having fired on their brothers.

Murder in those terrible days became a duty; the man who had not dipped his hands in proletarian blood became suspect in the eyes of the bourgeoisie. . . . At least the majority had the strength to be wicked, unlike those pathetic friends of the people, the orators, empty hearts! . . . Only one fearless lament, only one great cry of indignation was raised, and that was not in the Chamber. The sombre curse of the aged Lamennais will rest on the heads of the unfeeling cannibals and will sear with letters of shame the foreheads of the craven who, having uttered the word 'republic', became frightened of what it meant.

Paris! How long has this name shone like a guiding star to the peoples? Who did not love her, who did not bow down before her? But her time has passed. Away with her! In the June days she began a great struggle which she has not the power to resolve. Paris has grown old, and youthful dreams no longer become her. In order to gain new life she has need of powerful upheavals, Eves of St Bartholomew, September days. But the June horrors did not give her new life—where, then, will the decaying vampire draw new blood, the blood of the just, the blood that on June 27th reflected the lights of the street lanterns lit by the exulting bourgeoisie? Paris liked to play at soldiers; she made an Emperor out of a lucky soldier; she applauded the crimes called victory; she raised statues; fifteen years later she once again placed the bourgeois figure of the Little Corporal on a pillar; she translated the remains of the restorer of slavery with sacred awe. Even now she still hopes to find in soldiers the anchor of salvation from freedom and equality; she set savage hordes of barbarous Africans upon their brothers, so as not to have to go shares with them, and slaughtered them with the remorseless hands of a professional assassin. Then let her bear the consequences of her actions and her mistakes . . . Paris executed without trial. . . ? What will come of this blood? Who knows? But whatever comes, it is enough that in this orgy of madness, revenge, strife, retribution, the world will perish, the world in which the new man cannot breathe or live, which holds back the coming of the future. And that is excellent. Therefore long live chaos and destruction! *Vive la mort!* And may the future triumph!

PARIS, 1848
July 27th

III

YEAR LVII OF THE REPUBLIC, ONE AND INDIVISIBLE

Ce n'est pas le socialisme, c'est la république!

LEDRU-ROLLIN (*Speech in the Châlet*) *October 22nd, 1848*

A FEW days ago, the first Vendémiaire of the year 57 was celebrated. All the aristocrats of the democratic republic, all the bright red members of the Assembly, had gathered together in the Châlet on the Champs-Élysées. Towards the end of dinner Ledru-Rollin [1] delivered a brilliant speech. The speech full of *red* roses for the Republic and prickly thorns for the government, was a great success and fully deserved it. When he had finished, there were loud cries of '*Vive la République démocratique*!' Everyone stood up and very solemnly, with bared heads, sang the Marseillaise in unison. The words of Ledru-Rollin and the sound of the sacred song of liberation as well as the flowing wine made all faces glow. All eyes were ardent, and all the more so because not everything that was seething within found voice. The sound of drums coming from the camp on the Champs-Élysées was a reminder that the enemy was at hand, that the state of siege and the military dictatorship were not over.

Most of the guests were people in the prime of life,

[1] Alexandre-Auguste Ledru-Rollin (1808–74), radical lawyer and politician, one of the leaders of the republican opposition under Louis-Philippe. Elected Minister of the Interior in the Provisional Government of February 1848. Lost power after the June days. Tried to indict Louis-Napoleon May-June 1849. Escaped after subsequent insurrection, June 15th.

already with some experience of political affairs. They talked together loudly and vehemently. What energy, courage, nobility there is in the character of the French when the good elements of their nationality have not been smothered, but when they have torn themselves out of the mean and squalid bourgeois atmosphere which covers the whole of France like a green scum. What a manly, resolute expression there is upon their faces, what alacrity to translate words into action, to rush into battle, to face the enemy's bullets, to put or be put to death! I observed them for a long time and gradually an inexpressible sorrow rose up from the bottom of my soul and lay heavily on all my thoughts. I felt desperately sorry for this handful of men, noble, devoted, intelligent, gifted, the finest flower, perhaps, of the new generation. . . . Don't think that I was sorry for them because I felt that perhaps they might not survive until the first of Brumaire or the first of Nivôse of the year 57, because in a week, perhaps, they would die on the barricades, or perish in the galleys, in a penal colony, under the guillotine, or, perhaps, in the latest fashion, be shot down with their arms tied behind their backs, huddled into some corner of the Place du Carrousel or in the outer forts. All this is very sad, but it was not the cause of my sorrow; that lay deeper.

I was sorry for them because of the sincerity of their delusions, their honest belief in what could never be, their ardent faith as pure and as unreal as the chivalry of Don Quixote. I was sorry for them as a doctor might be sorry for a man who does not suspect the terrible disease within his breast. What moral suffering these men are preparing for themselves! They will fight like heroes, they will work all their lives and achieve nothing. They will give their blood, their strength, their lives, and when they grow old they will see that nothing has come of their labours, that they did not do what was wanted. They will die with a bitter disillusion in man, who is not really to blame, or—still worse—they will lapse back into childhood and will, as now, every day expect some enormous change, the establishment of *their* republic—mistaking the agonies of death for the pains of birth.

The Republic, as *they* conceive it, is an unrealizable abstraction, the fruit of theoretical reflections, the apotheosis of the existing state organization, the transfiguration of *what already exists*; their republic is the last dream, the poetic delirium of the old world. There is an element of prophecy in this delirium, but it is a prophecy concerning life beyond the grave, life in some future epoch. That is what they cannot understand, these men of the past, who, for all their revolutionary temper, remain tied to the old world, body and soul. They imagine that this decrepit world can, like Ulysses, regain its youth, unaware that the realization of one fraction of their republic would kill it instantly. They do not see that nothing could be more violently incompatible than their ideal and the existing order, that the one must die for the other to live. They cannot abandon the old forms; they regard them as eternal boundaries—that is why their ideal only bears the name and colour of the future, but in essence belongs to the world of the past and does not repudiate it.

Why are they not aware of this?

Their fatal error was that, carried away by a noble love for their neighbour, for freedom, carried away by impatience and indignation, they threw themselves into the task of liberating others before they had liberated themselves. They found enough strength to break their heavy iron chains, without noticing that the walls of the prison remained standing. They wanted to leave the walls as they were and to give them a new function—as though the plan of a prison could be adapted to a free life.

The old world, the Catholic-feudal world, has gone through all the changes of which it is capable. It has developed every side of itself, the most elegant and the most repellent, has made manifest all the truth that it contained, and all the falsehood; until it wore itself out. It can stand for some long time yet, but it cannot be renewed. The social consciousness now developing in it is such that every step towards its fulfilment means a way out of that world. A way out! Ah, there's the rub. For where can one go? What is there beyond its walls? Fear grips one—all is empty, vast, free. . . . How can one go without knowing where: how can one give up what one has, without any positive prospects? If Columbus had argued like this, he would never have weighed anchor. It was lunacy to sail the Ocean without knowing one's course, an Ocean on which no one had travelled before, and head for a country whose very existence was a question. By this lunacy he discovered a new world. Of course, if nations always moved from one set of furnished rooms to another—and always into a better set—things might be easier, but the trouble is that there is no one to prepare the new rooms. The future is worse than the Ocean—there is nothing there. It will be what men and circumstances make it.

If you are satisfied with the old world, try to preserve it. It is very frail and cannot last long under such shocks as those of February 24th. But if you find it intolerable to live in this state of perpetual conflict between beliefs and life, thinking one thing and doing another, leave the white-washed mediaeval cloister and risk the consequences. Audacity is on some occasions superior to profound wisdom. I know very well that this isn't easy; it is a serious matter for a man to part with everything that he has been used to all his life, with everything that he was born and bred with. Those of whom we speak are prepared for terrible sacrifices, but not those which a new life demands of them. Are they ready to sacrifice contemporary civilization, their way of life, religion, accepted conventional morality? Are they ready to lose all the fruits of civilization produced with such labour, fruits which of we have been boasting for three centuries and which are so dear to us? Are they willing to lose all the comforts and charms of our existence, to have barbarian youth rather than civilized senility, untilled soil and virgin forests instead of exhausted fields and artificial parkland? Will they demolish their ancestral castle for the sole pleasure of helping lay the foundations of a new house which will be built, no doubt, long after our day?

A madman's question, many will say. It was one put by Christ, but not in these words.

For a long time the liberals played happily with the idea of revolution, and the end of their play was February 24th. The popular hurricane swept them up to the top of a high steeple from which they could see where they were going and where they were leading others. Glancing down at the abyss that opened before their eyes, they grew pale. They saw that what was crumbling was not only what they had considered prejudice, but also everything else—what they had considered true and eternal. They were so terrified that some clutched at the falling walls, while others stopped half-way, repentant, and began to swear to all passers-by that this was not at all what they had wanted. This is why the men who proclaimed the republic became the assassins of freedom; this is why the liberal names that had resounded in our ears for a score of years or so, are today those of reactionary deputies, traitors, inquisitors. They want freedom and even a republic provided that it is confined to their own cultivated circle. Beyond the limits of their moderate circle they become conservatives. In the same way, rationalists were fond of explaining the mysteries of religion, they liked to reveal the meaning and essence of myths, they gave not a thought to where this would lead, nor did they suppose that their investigations, beginning with the fear of God, would end in atheism, that their criticism of church ritual would end in the denial of religion.

Since the Restoration liberals in all countries have called the people to the destruction of the monarchic and feudal order, in the name of equality, of the tears of the unfortunate, of the suffering of the oppressed, of the hunger of the poor. They have enjoyed hounding down various ministers with a series of impossible demands; they rejoiced when one feudal prop collapsed after another, and in the end became so excited that they outstripped their own desires. They came to their senses when, from behind the half-demolished walls, there emerged the proletarian, the worker with his axe and his blackened hands, hungry and half-naked in rags—not as he appears in books or in parliamentary chatter or in philanthropic verbiage, but in reality. This 'unfortunate brother' about whom so much has been said, on whom so much pity has been lavished, finally asked what was to be his share in all these blessings, where were *his* freedom, *his* equality, *his* fraternity? The liberals were aghast at the impudence and ingratitude of the worker. They took the streets of Paris by assault, they littered them with corpses, and then they hid from their *brother* behind the bayonets of martial law in their effort to save *civilization and order*!

They are right, but they are inconsistent. For in that case, why did they ever try to undermine the monarchy? How did they not see that in abolishing the monarchic principle the revolution could not stop at merely flinging out some dynasty or other? They were as happy as children because Louis-Philippe hadn't had time to reach St Cloud before there was a new government installed in the Hôtel de Ville and everything appeared to be taking its normal course—although the very smoothness of the upheaval should have opened their eyes to its unreality. The liberals were satisfied. But the people were not; and now they raised their voices, they echoed the words and promises of the liberals; but the liberals, like Peter, thrice denied their words and their promises, once they saw that things had taken a serious turn, and began the killing. In the same way Luther and Calvin drowned the anabaptists, the protestants repudiated Hegel, and the Hegelians Feuerbach. This is the position of *re-*

formers in general: all they do is to lay down the pontoons across which the peoples whom they have roused cross from one shore to the other. They like nothing better than the dreary, constitutional atmosphere of neither one being nor another. And it is in this world of logomachy, discord, irreconcilable contradictions, that these futile men wished, without changing it, to achieve their *pia desideria* of liberty, equality and fraternity.

The forms of European civil order, its civilization, its good and evil, are very different in their nature. They have developed from different principles and were shaped by different requirements. To a certain degree these forms, like everything living, were capable of change—but, like everything living, were changeable *only to a certain degree*; an organism can be trained, can deviate from its original function, can adapt itself to influences, until a point is reached when these deviations destroy its peculiarities, its individuality, that which constitutes its personality. When this happens, a struggle ensues and the organism either wins or perishes. The symptoms of death consist precisely in the fact that the constituent parts of the organism acquire new and different aims; they do not perish, but the personality does, while they enter into a series of quite different other relations and phenomena.

The state forms of France and other European countries are in their essence compatible with neither liberty, equality nor fraternity. If any of these ideas were realized, it would be the repudiation of contemporary European life; it would be its death. No constitution, no government is in a position to give feudal and monarchical countries true freedom and equality without annihilating everything feudal and monarchical in them. European life, Christian and aristocratic, has moulded our civilization, our notions, our ways of life. It cannot exist without a Christian and aristocratic environment. This environment can still evolve in keeping with the spirit of the times and the general level of education, and preserve its essence intact, in catholic Rome, in blaspheming Paris and in philosophising Germany alike; but further than this it cannot go without overstepping its frontiers. In some parts of Europe people can be a little freer than in others, a little more equal, but they cannot be really free, really equal as long as *this* civic framework exists, *this* civilization survives. All intelligent conservatives have known this, and that is why they support the old order with all their strength. Do you imagine for one moment that Metternich and Guizot did not see the injustices of the social order that surrounded them? But they saw also that these injustices were so much part of the organism as a whole that it needed only a touch and the whole edifice would come tumbling down. Realizing this, they became the guardians of the *status quo*. The liberals, on the other hand, have unleashed democracy and yet still want to return to the old order. Which of the two is nearer the truth?

In fact, of course, all of them are wrong—the Guizots and the Metternichs and the Cavaignacs. They all committed actual crimes for an imaginary aim; they oppressed, killed, shed blood, in order to arrest death. Neither Metternich with his intellect, nor Cavaignac with his soldiers, nor the republicans with their lack of understanding, can actually stop the stream with the current running so strong and fast. Only, instead of lending a helping hand, they strew the path of the people with broken glass. The people who walk on it will have a harder, a more difficult task; they will cut their feet, but they will pass along it all the same. The power of social ideas is great, especially since the true enemy has begun to understand it, the *de jure* enemy of the existing civil order: the proletarian, the worker, who in the past has reaped all the bitterness of this form of life and missed all its fruits. We may still regret the old order. Who should regret it if not we? It was good only to us. We grew up in it, we are its favoured sons; we admit that it ought to go, but we cannot withhold a tear. But the masses, crushed by toil, weakened by hunger, dulled by ignorance—what will they have to mourn at its funeral? They were the uninvited guests at the feast of life, as Malthus put it. Their *suppression* was a necessary condition of our lives.

All our education, our literary and scientific development, our love of beauty, our occupations, presuppose an environment constantly swept and tended by *others*, prepared by *others*; *somebody's* labour is essential in order to provide us with the leisure necessary for our mental development, that leisure, that active idleness which allows a thinker to concentrate, a poet to dream, an epicurean to enjoy himself, which ministers to the rich, luxurious, capricious, poetic development of our aristocratic personalities.

Who does not know the freshness of spirit created by carefree contentment? The poverty that produces a Gilbert [1] is an exception. Poverty dreadfully warps the human soul, no less than wealth. Anxiety about mere material cares crushes our capacities. But can well-being be within everyone's reach in the modern social order? Our civilization is a civilization of the minority—it is made possible only by the existence of a majority of proletarians. I am not a moralist, I am not sentimental; it seems to me that if in the past the minority really did lead spacious and agreeable lives and the majority remained silent, then this form of life was justified. I am not sorry for the twenty generations of Germans who were wasted in order to make Goethe possible, and am glad that the feudal dues of Pskov made it possible to rear Pushkin. Nature is merciless; like the notorious tree, she is at once a mother and a stepmother—she doesn't object to two-thirds of her creatures feeding the other third, as long as that other third does develop. If everyone cannot live well, let a few do so; let *one* man live

[1] Nicolas-Joseph-Laurent Gilbert (1751–80), French poet, traditionally said to have died in great poverty (in fact he died as a result of a fall from a horse).

at the cost of everyone else provided that he at least has a contented and easy life. This is the point of view from which one can understand aristocracy. For aristocracy is really a more or less civilized form of cannibalism: a savage who eats his prisoner, a landowner who draws an enormous rent from his estate, a manufacturer who grows rich at the expense of his workmen, are mere varieties of this same cannibalism. And incidentally I am ready to defend cannibalism in its crudest form. If one man thinks of himself as a dish and another wants to eat him, let him eat him. They both deserve it: the one to be a man-eater, the other to be his fodder.

So long as an educated minority, living off all previous generations, hardly guessed why life was so easy to live, so long as the majority, working day and night, did not quite realize why they received none of the fruits of their labour, both parties believed this to be the natural order of things, and the world of cannibalism could survive. People often take prejudice or habit for truth and in that case feel no discomfort: but if they once realize that their truth is nonsense, the game is up. From then onwards it is only by force that a man can be compelled to do what he considers to be absurd. Try and organize fasts without faith. It is out of the question. One would find it just as unbearable to eat Lenten food as a believer would to eat flesh.

Once the workers no longer want to work for another—that's the end of cannibalism, the point where aristocracy stops. The moment has been put off only because the workers have never calculated their strength properly and the peasants are backward in their education: but let them join forces and then you may bid farewell to your leisure, your luxury, your civilization; then the majority can no longer be expended in order to produce a brilliant luxurious life for the minority. In the realm of ideas, the exploitation of man by man is over, because no one any longer considers this relation to be just.

How can this world survive a social upheaval? In the name of what will it defend itself? Its religion is weakened, the monarchic principle has lost authority. It is preserved by fear and violence. The democratic principle is the cancer devouring it from within.

A heavy, dull, stifling, weary disgust with life is spreading, and at the same time spasmodic attempts are made to find a way out of it all. Life has become miserable for everyone—that is in itself a great symptom.

Where is the peaceful, contemplative, studious life, the life of the arts and sciences as the Germans used to know it? Where is that whirl of gaiety, wit, liberalism, elegance, music in which Paris moved? All that is past, out of mind. The last effort to rejuvenate the old world through its own resources has failed.

Everything shrinks and withers in this exhausted soil: there is no talent, no creation, no strength of mind, no strength of will. This world has outlived the age of its glory. The age of Schiller and Goethe has passed away, like the age of Raphael and Michelangelo, the age of Voltaire and Rousseau, of Mirabeau and Danton. The brilliant age of industry is over, like the brilliant age of aristocracy before it. Everyone is growing poorer, and no one the richer for it! All credit is at an end; people struggle on from one day to the next, the forms of life become less and less charming and graceful; people shrink into themselves, tremble and live like shop-keepers; the habits of the bourgeoisie have become universal. No one settles down, everything is temporary, borrowed, unstable. It is the same heavy atmosphere that oppressed people in the third century, when the very vices of ancient Rome were lost, when the emperors became dulled and the legions quietened down. Energetic and restless people suffered such depression that they fled in droves anywhere—to the steppes of the Thebaid, flinging down bags of gold on the public squares, and parting for ever from their country and their former gods.

Such a moment is not far from us: we are falling very low.

Repent, sirs, repent! Your day of judgment has arrived. You cannot save your world either by martial law or by a republic, or by executions, or by charities, or even by a redistribution of the land. Perhaps its fate would not have been so tragic had it not been defended so assiduously, so obstinately and with such a hopeless lack of imagination. No armistice will now help in France; antagonists cannot talk to one another nor understand one another; they do not use the same logic; their brains are different. When problems are posed like that there is no way out save battle; one or the other must fall; either monarchy or socialism.

Try and think which has the better chance. Myself I back socialism. That's hard to imagine, you may say. Well, it was hard to imagine that Christianity would triumph over Rome. I often imagine the clever conversations that Tacitus and Pliny had with their friends about that idiotic sect of Nazarenes, those Pierre-Leroux[1] who came out of Judaea with their vehement, half-demented speeches, or the Proudhon of those days,[2] who had come to Rome itself to preach the end of Rome. The empire stood in its pride and strength against those penniless propagandists, and yet it fell.

Or is it that you don't see the new Christians marching to build, the new barbarians marching to destroy? They are ready; like lava they are stirring heavily underground, in the bowels of the mountains. When the hour strikes, Herculaneum and Pompeii will be wiped out, the good and the bad, the innocent and the guilty will perish side by side. This will not be a judgment, not retribution, but a cataclysm, a total revolution. This lava, these barbarians, this new world, these Nazarenes, who are coming to finish off

[1]Pierre Leroux (1797–1871), Utopian socialist, publicist, and prophet, follower of Saint-Simon.

[2]i.e. St Paul.

all that is old and impotent and clear the path for the fresh and the new—they are nearer than you think. For it is they, none other, who are dying of hunger, of cold, it is they whose muttering we hear above us and below us, in garrets and in the cellars, while we sit on the *piano nobile*,

'over pastry and champagne'

talking of socialism. I know that this is nothing new, that it was like this before, but then people did not realize that this was very silly.

'But must the future form of life be brought about not by progress, but by the dark night of barbarism; must it be bought at a heavy loss?'

'I don't know, but I should have thought that if the educated minority lives to see this debacle and hasn't inoculated itself with the new notions, it will find life harder. Many people are indignant about this, but I find it comforting. To me these losses are proof that every historical phase has its complete reality, its own individuality, that each is an aim achieved, not a means. Therefore, each has its own virtue, its own good that is peculiar to it alone and that perishes along with it. Do you think the Roman patricians gained much, as far as their way of life was concerned, by conversion to Christianity? And did not the aristocrats before the revolution live better than you and I do now?'

'All that is so, but the thought of a rude and violent upheaval has for most people something repulsive about it. People who see that a change is imminent would yet like it to occur insensibly. Nature herself, they say, as she developed and grew richer and finer, ceased to have recourse to those dreadful cataclysms to which the earth's crust attests, filled as it is with the bones of whole populations that perished in these upheavals; since a more harmonious and peaceful metamorphosis is proper to that period of new development in which she has attained consciousness.'

'She has attained it only in a few heads, a small élite; the rest are still in the process of groping towards it and therefore still in the throes of *Naturgewalt*, instinct, dark forces and passion. In order that an idea which is clear and rational for you should also become someone else's idea, it is not enough that it should be true. The other's brain must be as well developed as yours, it must be emancipated from tradition. How will you persuade a workman to endure hunger and want while the social order changes by insensible degrees? How will you persuade a capitalist, a usurer, an owner to unclench the hand with which he clings to his monopolies and rights? It is hard to imagine such self-sacrifice. What could have been achieved has been achieved: the development of the middle class, a constitutional order, are nothing but the transitory forms linking the feudal-monarchic world with the social-republican one. The bourgeoisie precisely represents this semi-liberation, this impudent onslaught on the past made with the desire to inherit its power. It was working for itself and was right to do so. A man really does something serious only when he does it for himself. The bourgeoisie could not after all see itself as a mere hideous intermediate link. It conceived of itself as an end; but since its moral principle was meaner and poorer than what there was in the past—whereas development becomes faster and faster—it is not surprising that the world of the bourgeoisie has exhausted itself so soon and has no capacity for self-renewal. And anyway, how, according to you, is the upheaval to take place by insensible degrees? By the splitting up of property, as was done during the first revolution? The result of this would be general squalor. The small proprietor is the worst bourgeois of all. All the forces now locked in the long-suffering but powerful brain of the proletarian would be dissipated. It is true that he would not die of starvation, but that would be all. He would still be cramped on his small parcel of land, or in his garret in the workers' barracks. Such is the prospect of a peaceful organic revolution. If this takes place, the main current of history will find another bed; it will not get lost in sand and clay, like the Rhine. Humanity will not follow a narrow and dirty track—it demands a broad avenue. And it will stop at nothing in order to create it.'

In nature conservatism is just as powerful as the revolutionary element. Nature allows the old and the useless to live on, but she did not spare the mammoths and the mastodons when she was arranging the world. The revolution that destroyed them was not directed *against* them; if they could have escaped it they would have survived and then quietly and peacefully degenerated in an unpropitious environment. The mammoths whose skin and bones are found frozen in Siberia probably escaped the geological revolution; they are the Comneni, the Paleologoi of the feudal world. Nature has nothing against that, any more than history. We superimpose upon her a sentimental personality and our passions; we become oblivious to our metaphors, and take the turns of phrase we use for reality. Unaware of the absurdity of it, we introduce our own petty household rules into the economy of the universe for which the life of generations, peoples, of entire planets, has no importance in relation to the general development. In contrast to us, who are subjective and love only what is personal, for Nature the death of the individual is the fulfilment of the same necessity, of the same play of life as his birth; she does not lament his passing, for change as it may, nothing escapes her large embrace.

CHAMPS ÉLYSÉES, 1848
October 1st

IV

VIXERUNT!

Vanquished death with death
Matins—Easter Sunday

ON November 20th,[1] 1848, the weather in Paris was abominable; for the first time since summer there was a biting wind and early snow and frost to remind one of the approach of winter. People here dread the winter as a public calamity; the poor prepare to shiver in their unheated attics, without warm clothes, without enough food; the death rate goes up during these two months of ice, sleet and damp; the workers are worn out by fever which leaves them without strength.

On that day dawn never broke; the wet snow fell steadily, thawing in the misty air; the wind tore at people's hats and viciously flapped the hundreds of tricolours tied to tall masts near the Place de la Concorde. Large numbers of soldiers and National Guards were standing around packed tight together; a kind of structure with a Christian cross on the top had been put up at the entrance to the Tuileries gardens; from the Gardens to the Obelisk the square surrounded by soldiers was empty. The line regiments, the Garde Mobile, the lancers, the dragoons, the artillery, filled all the streets leading to the square. An ignorant observer could never have guessed the purpose of all these preparations. Was it another royal execution? Was it to be an announcement that France was in danger? No, it was a

[1]The events described here in fact took place on November 12th.

January 21st—not for the King, but for the people, for the revolution. February 24th was being buried.

About nine in the morning, an ill-assorted group of elderly persons began to make their way across the bridge. They shuffled along despondently, their coat collars turned up, feeling uncertainly for a dry patch on which to step. Two leaders walked in front. One of them was muffled in an African cloak, which all but hid the harsh, stern features of a mediaeval condottiere; in his haggard, emaciated face there was nothing human to soften the likeness to a bird of prey; his frail figure breathed disaster and misfortune. The other, plump, and elaborately dressed, with curly grey hair, wore nothing over his frock-coat; he walked with studied and insolent casualness, and his once handsome face revealed nothing except a conscious, almost sensual pleasure in his own dignity and importance.

There was no greeting to welcome them, only the obedient bark of the guns and the presented arms. At the same moment, from the opposite side, from the Madeleine, another group of men appeared, looking even stranger, in mediaeval garb, in mitres and surplices, surrounded by acolytes carrying censers. With their rosaries and their missals they looked like long dead and forgotten shadows of the feudal age.

What were they doing, these two groups?

One group was going to proclaim, under the protection of a hundred thousand bayonets, the *will of the people*, a statute composed under fire and discussed during a state of siege, in the name of *liberty*, *equality and fraternity*; the other was going to bless this fruit of philosophy and revolution in the name of *the Father*, *the Son and the Holy Ghost*.

The people did not even turn out to look at this parody. In sad knots they were strolling around the communal grave of their brothers who had fallen for them by the June column! It was the small shopkeepers, pedlars, salesmen, concierges of the neighbouring houses, waiters and people like us, foreign tourists, who formed the line behind the regular troops and the armed bourgeoisie. But even these spectators looked on with amazement at the public proclamation, which was quite inaudible; at the fancy dress of the judges—red and black, with fur and without fur—at the snow which cut at one's eyes, at the martial array of troops, to whom a rather grim air was lent by the shooting that came from the esplanade of the Invalides. The soldiers and the shots reminded one instinctively of the June days, and one's heart grew taut within one. All faces looked worried, as though everyone was conscious of doing wrong —some because they were committing a crime, others because they were involved in it by permitting it. At the slightest noise or rustle thousands of heads turned round expecting to hear the whistle of a bullet, the shout of rebellion, the measured sound of the tocsin. The snowstorm raged on. The troops, wet to the skin, began to grumble. At last the drums beat; the crowd started, and an endless procession set off to the feeble sounds of *Mourir pour la patrie*, which had now replaced the great Marseillaise.

Just then the young man with whom we are already acquainted made his way through the crowd towards a middle-aged man and said to him with signs of genuine delight, 'What an unexpected pleasure! I didn't know you were here.'

'Ah, how are you?' the man replied, extending both hands in friendly fashion. 'Have you been here long?'

'I arrived a few days ago.'

'From where?'

'Italy.'

'Well, what's it like there? Awful?'

'Don't let's talk of it. . . . Terrible.'

'Well, well, my dear idealistic dreamer I always knew that the February ordeal would be too much for you and that you were storing up for yourself a good deal of pain—

pain is always the measure of one's hopes . . . you all complained of stagnation in Europe. You can scarcely reproach it with that now, can you?'

'Don't laugh. There are circumstances about which it's wrong to laugh, however much scepticism there may be in your soul. When one can't cry enough—is that the time to mock? I must admit that as far as I'm concerned, I'm terrified of looking back, terrified of remembering! It is hardly a year since we parted, but it feels like a hundred years. To see all one's finest hopes, all one's innermost aspirations being realized, to see the possibility of their fulfilment—and then to fall so low, so far! To lose everything, and not in battle, not in a struggle with the enemy, but by one's own impotence and ineptitude. That's what's terrible. I'm ashamed to meet a legitimist; they laugh in one's face, and I feel they're right. What a school—not for progress but for the blunting of all one's faculties! I am terribly glad to have run into you. I'd reached the stage when it became imperative for me to see you. I've often quarrelled with you in absence, and made it up. I even wrote you an enormous letter one day, and am now glad enough that I tore it up. It was filled with the most arrogant hopes, I was intending to shatter you with them. And now all that I want is for you finally to convince me that this world is perishing, that it has no way out, that it is doomed to become parched and everything in it to run to seed. Now you won't be able to upset me, and indeed I didn't ever expect our meeting to bring relief; what you say always makes me feel gloomier and not more cheerful—and that's exactly what I want! Convince me, and I go to Marseilles tomorrow and take the first boat to America or Egypt—anything to get out of Europe. I'm tired, I'm at the end of my tether here. My heart and my mind are sick. I shall go mad if I stay on.'

'There are few nervous disorders more recalcitrant than idealism. I find you after all that has just happened the same as I left you. You would rather suffer than understand. Idealists are terribly spoilt and great cowards—I've had to apologize before for this expression. You know that I'm not talking of personal courage; of that there's almost too much. Idealists are cowards about facing the truth; you push it away, you're afraid of facts that don't fit your theories. You believe that there is no salvation for the world except along the paths you have found. What you want is that the world should, out of gratitude for your devotion, dance to your tune, and, as soon as you realize that it has its own step and rhythm, you feel angry; you're cross, you despair. You haven't enough curiosity to watch it doing its own dance.'

'Call it what you like, cowardice or stupidity—but it's true that I'm not interested in watching this *danse macabre*. I don't share the Roman passion for disgusting spectacles, perhaps because I don't understand all the subtleties of the art of dying.'

'Whether curiosity is worthy or not depends on the quality of the spectacle. The audience in the Colosseum was the same idle crowd as that which thronged to the *autos da fé* and the executions, or that which came here today in search of something to fill its inner void, or that which tomorrow will go with the same eagerness to watch one of today's heroes being hanged. But there is another, a worthier kind of curiosity—its roots are in a healthier soil, it leads to knowledge, and inquiry. It's the sort that's always tormented by questions about any unexplored part of the world, and will expose itself to an infection in order to learn the properties of that infection.'

'In short, the kind that aims at the useful; but what use can there be in watching a dying man, when you know that it is too late to help him? That is simply the poetry of curiosity.'

'For me this poetic curiosity, as you call it, is exceedingly human. I admire Pliny who remained in his boat, oblivious of manifest danger, to watch the mighty eruption of

Vesuvius to the end. To withdraw would have been more sensible and certainly safer.'

'I understand the hint, but the parallel doesn't quite fit. At the destruction of Pompeii there was nothing that a man could do. Whether to watch or go away was a matter for him. I'm not trying to avoid danger. I want to go because I cannot stay any longer. To face danger is much easier than it may seem from afar, but to watch destruction with hands folded knowing that you can be of no use; understanding what needs to be done but unable to communicate your knowledge, to point out, to explain; looking idly on while people, convulsed by some general madness, run amok and destroy each other in frenzy, while an entire civilization, a whole world, is collapsing, amidst chaos and ruin—that is beyond human powers. There is nothing to be done about Vesuvius, but in the world of history man is at home; he is not only a spectator but an actor; here he has a voice and if he cannot take part, he should at least protest by his absence.'

'Yes, man is at home in history, but from your words one might gather that he is only a guest in nature, as though there were a stone wall between nature and history. I believe that he is at home in both, but in neither of them an absolute master. The reason why man does not feel insulted by the insubordination of nature is that her autonomy is manifest to him. We believe in her reality, independent of ourselves, but in the reality of history, particularly of contemporary history, we do not believe. In history man appears to have complete freedom to do what he likes. All this is the bitter consequence of that dualism which for so long has made us see double and waver between two optical illusions. Now the dualism is less crude but it still lingers unnoticed in our souls. Our language, our first notions, which become natural by force of habit, by repetition, prevent us from seeing the truth. If we had not learnt from the age of five that nature and history are two different things, it would not have been difficult for us to understand that the development of nature passes imperceptibly into the development of mankind, that these are two chapters of one novel, two phases of one process, very far apart at the extremities, very close together in the centre. It would not have surprised us, then, that part of everything that takes place in history is influenced by physiology, by dark forces. It is true that the laws of historical development are not opposed to the laws of logic, but their paths do not coincide with those of thought, just as nothing in nature coincides with the abstract norms constructed by pure reason. Knowing all this, we would have striven to study, to discover these physiological influences. But do we do so? Has anyone ever given serious thought to the physiology of social life, of history as a truly objective science? No one: neither conservatives, nor radicals, nor philosophers, nor historians.'

'Nevertheless there has been a great deal of action, because it is perhaps as natural for us to make history as it is for a bee to make honey, because to do so is not the fruit of reflection, but the inner necessity of the human spirit.'

'By that you mean instinct. You are right. It is instinct that has led and still leads the masses. But we are not in the same position, we have lost the primeval sureness of instinct, we have become so introspective that we have killed in ourselves those natural impulses by means of which history fights its way forward into the future. We are, on the whole, city dwellers who have lost both the physical and the moral sense—the farmer and the sailor can foretell the weather, but we cannot. All that is left to us in the way of instinct is a restless desire to be active—and that is excellent. A conscious action, i.e. one that would completely satisfy us, cannot yet exist. We are still groping our way. We try to impose our wishes, our thoughts, on our surroundings, and these attempts, always unsuccessful, serve to educate us. You are irritated because the nations don't fulfil the conception that is dear and clear to you, because they are unable to save themselves with the weapons you offer them and to cease suffering. But why do you think that the nation is obliged to fulfil your conception and not its own, and precisely at this time, and not another? Are you sure that the means you have invented have no drawbacks? Are you sure that it understands them, that there is no other method, no wider aims? You may, indeed, have grasped correctly its conception—it would be by a mere stroke of luck—but more likely you are mistaken. You and the masses belong to two different cultures. There are centuries between you, greater than the oceans that are now crossed so easily. The masses are full of secret aspirations and passionate impulses, their thought has not become divorced from fantasy, nor does it remain theory with them as it does with us; in their case it immediately turns to action—that is why it is difficult to impregnate the masses with ideas because for them ideas are not something frivolous. That is why they sometimes outstrip the most daring thinkers and make them follow on behind unwillingly, sometimes desert midway those whom yesterday they adored, sometimes lag behind others against all probability. They are children, women; they are capricious, violent and fickle. Instead of studying this unique physiology of the human race, instead of conforming to it, of trying to understand its ways and its laws, we begin to criticize, to instruct, to be indignant and angry as though the people and nature were responsible, as though they were in the least concerned whether we like their life or not, a life which draws them irresistibly towards vague aims and irresponsible acts. Up to now, this didactic, pontifical attitude had its justification, but now it has become ridiculous and casts us for the stock role of the disillusioned. You are offended by what is going on in Europe, you are outraged by this cruel, dull, triumphant reaction; so am I; but you, faithful to romanticism, are angry and want to run away, so as to avoid seeing the truth. I agree that it is time to abandon our artificial conventional life, but not by escaping to America. What do you expect to find there? The United States is the last, well-produced edition of the same feudal-Christian text and, what is more, in a crude English translation. A year ago, your departure would have had nothing astonishing about it. Things were dragging on in a slow, limp fashion. But how can you go at the very height of the débâcle, when everything in Europe is fermenting, seething; when ancient walls are tumbling down, when one idol falls after another, when people have learnt to build barricades in Vienna?'

'And when, to complete the picture, they have learnt to break them with shells in Paris, when together with the idols—which, by the way, go up again, the next day—fall for ever the finest fruits of European life, cultivated and grown with such difficulty over the centuries. I see judgment, execution, death, but I can see neither resurrection nor mercy. This part of the world has done what it had to do; now its strength is exhausted. The people living in this zone have accomplished their mission, they grow dull and backward. The stream of history has, evidently, found another bed—that is where I am going. You yourself said something to me along those lines last year—do you remember—on the boat—when we were travelling from Genoa to Cività?'

'I remember. It was *before the storm.* Only then you disagreed with me and now you agree too much. You have come to your new point of view not by experience, nor by thought. That is why, with you, instead of having a calm character, it is frenzied; you have come to it *par dépit*, because of a momentary despair which you have naively, unthinkingly, drawn over past hopes. If this point of view of yours were not the tantrums of a sulky lover, but a sober realization of what is happening, you would have expressed yourself differently, envisaged things differently, you would have abandoned all personal *rancune*, you would have forgotten yourself, you would have been moved and terrified by the tragic fate that is being enacted before your eyes. But idealists are chary of surrendering themselves; they are just as stubbornly egotistical as monks who can stand any privations but never forget themselves, their personality, the reward. Why are you afraid of staying here? Do you leave the theatre at the beginning of the fifth act of every tragedy because you are afraid that your nerves will be upset? The fate of Oedipus will be no better if you leave the stalls; he will perish just the same. It is better to remain to the end of the performance; sometimes a spectator, broken by Hamlet's misfortune, meets the young Fortinbras full of life and hope. The spectacle of death in itself is solemn; it carries a deep message. The cloud that hung over Europe, allowing no one to breathe freely, has burst; lightning flash after flash, thunder clap on thunder clap; the earth trembles, and you want to run away because Radetsky has taken Milan and Cavaignac Paris. This is what comes from not recognizing the objectivity of history. I detest humility, but in such cases as the present humility means understanding; this is the moment to be humble before history, to recognize it. Moreover, things are going better than could have been expected. So what are you angry about? We were preparing to wither, to fade away in the sickly, debilitating atmosphere of gradual senility, when, instead of a lingering corruption, Europe fell ill with typhus: she is collapsing, falling to pieces, melting away, losing consciousness—losing it to such a degree that in her struggles both sides grow mad and understand neither the enemy nor themselves. The fifth act of the tragedy began on February 24th; gloom and restlessness of spirit are quite natural; no serious person will cast taunts in the face of such events, but this is remote from your despair and your point of view. You imagine that you despair because you are a revolutionary, and you are mistaken. You despair because you are a conservative.'

'Thank you very much. So, according to you, I am no better than Radetsky and Windischgrätz?'[1]

'Certainly not: you are much worse. What sort of a conservative is Radetsky? He destroys everything; he nearly blew up the Cathedral in Milan. Do you seriously consider it conservatism when wild Croats overrun Austrian towns and don't leave stone on stone? Neither they nor their generals know what they're doing, but whatever it is, it is not "conserving". You judge everybody by their labels—those who are for the Emperor are conservatives, those who are for the republic are revolutionaries. But to-day the principles of monarchy and conservatism are to be found fighting on both sides alike. The most noxious conservatism is the one that is on the side of the republic, the one that you preach.'

'It really might help if you explained what it is that I am trying to preserve, where exactly it is that you find my revolutionary conservatism.'

'Well then, tell me, aren't you annoyed that the constitution that is being proclaimed to-day is so stupid?'

'Yes, of course.'

'You are angry at the fact that the movement in Germany went up in smoke through the Frankfort chimney, that Charles Albert didn't safeguard the independence of Italy, that Pius IX turned out to be totally worthless?'

'Yes, but what of it? I don't deny it.'

'But this is what conservatism is. If your wishes had been fulfilled, the result would have been the solemn exculpation of the old world. Everything would have emerged with flying colours, except the revolution.'

'So now we really ought to be glad that the Austrians have conquered Lombardy?'

'Why glad? Neither be glad nor be surprised. Lombardy couldn't be freed by demonstrations in Milan and the help of Charles Albert.'[2]

[1]Prince Alfred Windischgrätz (1787–1862). Suppressed rebellions in Austria and Bohemia 1848.

[2]Of Savoy.

'It's all very well for us to discuss this *sub specie aeternitatis*. Nevertheless, I know how to distinguish man from his dialectic. I am certain that you would have forgotten all your theories if you had seen the piles of corpses, and the plundered towns, and the ravished women, and the brutal soldiers in their white uniforms.'

'Instead of replying, you appeal to sentiment, which is always effective. Everybody, except a moral monster, has a heart. It is as easy to arouse pity with the fate of Milan as it is with that of the Duchesse de Lamballe.[1] Compassion is natural to man. Surely you don't believe like Lucretius that nothing is more delightful than to stand in safety on the shore and watch a sinking ship? That is a poet's slander. Chance victims struck down by brute force shock our whole moral being. I didn't see Radetsky in Milan, but I saw the plague in Alexandria. I know how these fatal scourges destroy and humiliate man, but to stop at tears is poor, weak. With indignation there is born an unconquerable desire to resist, to fight, to explore, to discover remedies and causes. Sensibility will not solve these matters. Doctors discuss the condition of a man who is seriously ill in a manner very different from his inconsolable relations. They may weep in their hearts and feel sympathy, but to fight the disease one needs knowledge, not tears. Above all, much as a doctor may feel affection for his patient, he must never lose his head, never be surprised by the approach of death, the imminence of which he has already recognized. Though if you are mourning *only* the actual people who perish in this appalling ferment and disaster, you are right. Insensibility requires training; people who have no fellow-feeling for their neighbour—generals, ministers, judges and hangmen

[1]Marie Thérèse Louise, Princesse de Lamballe (1748–92), close friend of Marie-Antoinette. At the outbreak of the revolution, came to England to win sympathy for royal cause. Returned to France to rejoin the queen, was imprisoned in La Force, August 1792, and then handed over to the mob who brutally killed her, September 3rd.

—have trained themselves all their lives to be inhuman. Had they not succeeded in this they could never have gone on. Your sorrow is wholly justified and I have no consolation to offer, other than a quantitative one. Remember that all the events from the revolt in Palermo to the occupation of Vienna cost Europe less than a third of the men killed, for instance, at Eylau. Our notions are still so confused that we don't know how to count the fallen, if they fall as soldiers, brought there not by the desire to fight, not by conviction, but by the social plague called recruitment. Those who fell at the barricades at least knew what they were dying for; but, as for the others, if they could only have heard how the famous river meeting between the two Emperors began, they would have had to blush for their courage. "What are we fighting over?" asked Napoleon, "It is all a misunderstanding." "Quite true; over nothing at all," replied Alexander. And they embraced. Tens of thousands of soldiers killed tens of thousands of other soldiers with exemplary bravery, and left their bones on the battlefield *because of a misunderstanding*. However that may be, whether many people were killed or few, I repeat; one is sorry for them, very sorry. But it seems to me that you are mourning not only these people, but also something else as well?'

'A very great deal else. I mourn the revolution of February 24th which started so magnificently and perished so humbly. The republic was possible. I saw it, I breathed its air, the republic was not a dream, but a reality. What came of it? I'm sorry for it, as sorry as I am for Italy, which woke up one day only to be conquered the next, or as I am for Germany which rose to its full height only to fall at the feet of its thirty squires. I'm sorry that humanity has again gone back a whole generation, that its movement is again strangled, arrested.'

'As far as the movement itself is concerned, that cannot be tamed. The motto of our age, more than of any other is "*semper in motu*". . . . You see how right I was when I reproached you for conservatism. This element is so strong in you that it leads you to contradictions. Was it not you who spoke to me a year ago about the terrible moral collapse of the educated classes in France? And now you suddenly believe that they could have been transformed overnight into republicans, just because the people sent a stubborn old man [1] packing and replaced an obstinate Quaker [2] and his crew of minor diplomats with a spineless neo-philanthropist [3] and his crew of minor journalists.'

'It is easy to be wise after the event.'

'And it wasn't very difficult to be so before: February 26th determined the character of the 24th. All non-conservatives understood that this republic was a play on words: Blanqui and Proudhon, Raspail and Pierre Leroux. No prophetic gift was needed, just the habit of conscientious research, the habit of observation. That is why I recommend the natural sciences to you for exercising and sharpening the brain. The naturalist is used to watching and waiting and not introducing anything of his own until the time comes to do so. He will not miss a single symptom, a single change; he seeks truth disinterestedly, without colouring it with either his love or his hate. Remember that the most penetrating pamphleteer of the first revolution was a veterinary surgeon [4] and that it was a chemist [5] who on February 27th printed in his journal (which was burnt by students in the Latin Quarter) facts of which everyone is now aware but which it is now too late to mend. It was unforgivable to expect anything from the political surprise of February 24th except ferment; and it began on that very day and is its greatest achievement; one cannot deny this ferment. It is drawing France and the whole of Europe from upheaval to upheaval. Was that what you wanted, what you expected? No, you expected that the sensible republic

[1] Louis-Philippe. [2] Guizot. [3] Lamartine.
[4] Jean Paul Marat. [5] Raspail.

would stand on its rickety legs of Lamartinean unction, swathed in the bulletins of Ledru-Rollin. This would have been a universal catastrophe; such a republic would have been the strongest brake on the wheels of history. A Republic of the Provisional Government, based on old monarchical principles, would have been worse than any monarchy. It presented itself not as stupid brute force, but as a free act of consent; not as an historical disaster but as something rational, just, with its crass majority and its lying slogans. The word "republic" had a moral power which no throne possesses any longer. Deceiving everyone by its name, it provided buttresses for a crumbling political order. The reaction saved the movement, the reaction tore off the masks and thereby saved the revolution. People who would have remained for years drugged with the laudanum of Lamartine came to their senses after three months of martial law; now they know what it means to suppress mutiny according to the principles of *this* republic. Things that were clear only for a few have become apparent to all; everyone knows that it was not Cavaignac who was to blame for what happened; to blame the executioner is stupid, he is disgusting rather than guilty. Without knowing what it was doing the reaction cut down the last idols, behind which, as behind the altar, the old order was hiding. The people no longer believe in the republic, and that's excellent. It's time to stop believing in one, sole, saving Church. The religion of the republic was in place in '93; then it was colossal, great. It produced that noble line of giants with whom the long era of political revolutions comes to an end. The formal republic appeared in its true colours after the June days. The incompatibility of fraternity or equality with the snares called assizes of freedom or the slaughter-houses that go by the name of military tribunals, is beginning to dawn upon many. No one believes any longer in these packed juries which decide men's fate blindfold and allow no appeal; nor in the social order that protects only property, that deports people as a measure of public safety, that keeps a standing army, be it only a hundred men, which is always ready to pull the trigger at the first command, without asking why. These are the contributions of reaction. Doubts are stirring and force men to think, and it was no easy task to do this, especially with Frenchmen who, in spite of their acumen, are very impervious to anything new. It was the same in Germany: at first it was all a success in Berlin and Vienna—people seemed delighted with their Diets, their Charters, for which they had yearned timidly for thirty-five years. Now, having experienced reaction and knowing by experience what Diets and Chambers of Deputies mean, they will not be satisfied with any Charter, neither granted nor taken. Charters have become for the Germans what a toy is for a man who dreamt of it as a child. Europe has realized, thanks to the reaction, that a representative system is a cunning device to transmute social needs and a readiness for energetic action into words and endless arguments. Instead of being glad about all this, you are indignant. You are indignant because the National Assembly, composed of reactionaries, endowed with absurd powers and motivated by cowardice, voted for an absurdity. But in my opinion that is an outstanding proof that all these Oecumenical Councils for legislation, all these representatives posing as high priests, are quite unnecessary and that at present it is impossible to vote an intelligent constitution. Is it not ridiculous to make laws for the generations to come, when the decrepit world has barely time to make dispositions for the future or to dictate any sort of will? The reason why you do not applaud all these failures is that you are a conservative, because consciously or unconsciously you belong to the existing world. Last year, angry and indignant with it, you did not leave it. In return, it deceived you with February 24th. You believed that it could be saved by internal remedies, agitation, reforms; you believed it could be rejuvenated, and yet remain as it was; you believed it *could* be reformed and you still believe this. A few street riots, Ledru-Rollin declared president of France, and you would again be in ecstasy. When you are young, this is excusable, but I don't advise you to go on like this for long. You'll make a fool of yourself. You have a lively, impressionable nature. Jump the last hurdle, shake the last speck of dust off your boots, and realize that small revolutions, small changes, small republics are not enough, their influence is too limited, they cease to have any point. Don't fall for them—they are all infected with conservatism. Of course, I want to be fair to them, for they have their good points. Life in Rome is better under Pius IX than it was under the drunken and nasty Gregory XVI. Again, the Republic of February 26th in some respects offers a better form for the development of new ideas than the monarchy, but all these palliatives are as noxious as they are useful. The momentary relief makes one forget the disease itself. But then, when one examines these improvements closer to and sees with what a sour, discontented face they are made, how every small concession is represented as a virtuous action, how reluctantly, how offensively they are granted—then, surely, one is no longer inclined to overestimate their value. I don't know how to choose between kinds of slavery any more than between religions. My palate becomes dulled. I am incapable of subtle distinctions, of deciding which slavery is worse, which better, which religion is nearer to salvation, and which further away: which is more oppressive, an honest republic or an honest monarchy, the revolutionary conservatism of Radetsky or the conservative revolutionism of Cavaignac: who are more repellent, the Quakers or the Jesuits: what is worse, the whip or the *crapaudine*.[1] On both sides there is slavery: on the one side it is sly, concealed under the name of liberty and therefore dangerous: on the other side, it is wild and bestial, therefore quite open.

[1] A punishment inflicted in the French army in Algiers.

Luckily, neither side recognizes the family resemblances in the other, and both are ready to fight at any moment. Well, let them fight, let them form coalitions, let them snap at each other, and drag each other to the grave. Whichever comes out the victor, falsehood or violence, the victory is not for us—nor, incidentally, for them either. All that the conquerors will succeed in doing is to contrive to live well for a day or two.'

'And we are to remain spectators as before, eternal spectators, miserable members of a jury, whose verdict is never accepted, experts whose testimony no one wants. I am surprised at you and don't know whether to envy you or not. For someone with such an active brain you have so much—how shall I put it?—so much restraint.'

'I can't help it. I don't wish to force myself; sincerity and independence are my gods. I have no desire to march under the one banner or the other. Both sides are so well on the road to the grave that they don't need any help from me. There have been similar situations in the past. What sort of part could Christians play in the struggles that went on in Rome between the various pretenders to the Imperial throne? They were called cowards. They smiled, and went on with their own work, praying and preaching.'

'They preached because they were strong in their faith. They had a unity of doctrine. Where is our gospel? Where is the new life to which we call people, the good tidings to which we are called upon to bear witness?'

'Preach the tidings of death, show people every new sore on the breast of the old world, every victory of destruction. Show the feebleness of its efforts, the meanness of its ambitions; show that it cannot recover, that it has no support and no faith in itself, that no one really loves it, that it rests on misunderstandings; show that every victory is at the same time a self-inflicted wound; preach death as the good tidings of the coming redemption.'

'Would it not be better to pray? Who is there to preach

to when the victims are falling on both sides? There was once a bishop in Paris who didn't realize that people don't listen in the middle of a battle. Let us wait a little. When the battle is over, then let's start our sermons about death. There will be no one to stop us in the large graveyard where all the fighters will lie down side by side. Who better than the dead to listen to the apotheosis of death? If matters proceed as they do now, it will be a novel spectacle. The rising future will perish together with the dying old world. Untried democracy will wither, wounding the cold, emaciated breast of the dying monarchy.'

'A future that perishes is not a future. Democracy is essentially the present: it is a struggle, a denial of hierarchy, of the social lie that has grown up in the past, a purifying flame which will burn up all the obsolete forms and will of course die down when all is consumed. Democracy can create nothing, creation is not its business. It will become meaningless after the death of its last enemy. *Democrats,* (to quote Cromwell), *know only what they do not want; what they want, they do not know.*'

'Behind the knowledge of what we do not want there lurks a sense of what we do want. This forms the basis of the idea which has been repeated so often that one can hardly repeat it; that every destruction is in its way a creation. Man cannot be satisfied with mere destruction. It is contrary to his creative nature. To preach death, he needs faith in a new birth. It was easy for Christians to announce the end of the old world; for with them the funeral was to coincide with the baptism.'

'We have something more than a mere sense of the future, but we are not so easily satisfied as the Christians. They had only one criterion, and that was faith. The unshakable conviction that the Church would triumph and that the world would be baptized was for them, of course, an immense source of comfort. It never entered their heads that the baptized child would not turn out entirely in accordance with the wishes of its godparents. Christianity has remained a pious hope. Now, on the eve of death, as in the first century, it comforts itself with heaven, paradise; it would be lost without heaven. To instil the idea of a new life is an incomparably harder task in our age. We have no heaven, no "God's abode". Our abode is a human one and has to find its fulfilment on the soil on which everything real exists, on the earth. Here we cannot plead temptation by the devil, or God's help, or life after death. Democracy, anyway, does not go so far—it is still on the Christian shore. It has a vast fund of ascetic romanticism, of liberal idealism. It has a terrifying power of destruction, but as soon as it starts to create, it gets lost in school-boy experiments, in political exercises. Of course, destruction creates: it clears the ground, and that is already creation; it removes many falsehoods, and that already is truth. But there is no real creation in democracy, and that is why it is not the future. The future is outside politics, the future soars above the chaos of all political and social aspirations and picks out from them threads to weave into a new cloth which will provide the winding-sheet for the past and the swaddling clothes for the new-born. Socialism corresponds to the Nazarene teaching in the Roman Empire.'

'If one recalls what you said just now about Christianity and one extends the parallel, the future of Socialism is not an enviable one. It will remain an eternal hope.'

'And in the process will develop a brilliant era of history under its blessing. The Gospels were not fulfilled and there was no need for that—but what were fulfilled were the Middle Ages, and the ages of reconstruction and the ages of revolution, and Christianity penetrated all these manifestations, participated in everything, acted as guide and pilot. The fulfilment of socialism involves the same unexpected combination of abstract doctrine and existing fact. Life realizes only that aspect of an idea which falls on favourable soil, and the soil in this case doesn't remain a mere passive medium, but gives its sap, contributes its own elements. The new element born of the conflict between Utopias and conservatism enters life, not as the one or as the other side expected it—it enters transformed, different, composed of memories and hopes, of existing things and things to be, of traditions and pledges, of belief and science, of Romans who have lived too long, and Germans who have not lived at all, united by one church, alien to both. Ideals, theoretical constructions, never materialize in the shape in which they float in our minds.'

'Why and wherefore, then, if this is so, do they come into our heads at all? It's a sort of irony.'

'Why do you want everything in a man's brain to fit precisely? What a pedestrian reduction of everything to bare necessity, to the narrowly utilitarian, to the obviously practical. Remember old Lear who, when one of his daughters reduced his state, declaring that it would suffice for his needs, said to her:

> 'O, reason not the need: our basest beggars
> Are in the poorest thing superfluous:
> Allow not nature more than nature needs.
> Man's life is cheap as beast's. . . .'

Man's thoughts and fancy are incomparably freer than people think. Entire worlds of poetry, lyricism and meditation, independent, to some degree, of surrounding circumstances, lie dormant in everyone's soul. A jolt rouses them and they wake up with their visions, their decisions, their theories. Thought, leaning on firm fact, strives to attain universal norms, to escape from casual and provisional definitions into the realm of logic, but from this realm to the practical is very far.'

'Listening to your words, I was wondering how it is that you have so strong a sense of impartial justice. I have discovered the reason. You have not been hurled into the stream, you have not been sucked into this whirlpool. A stranger can always unravel family problems better than any member of the family. But if, like so many others, like Barbès, like Mazzini, you had toiled all your life because within your soul there was a voice calling you to this action, a voice which you were unable to shout down because it rose from the depths of a humiliated heart, bleeding at the sight of oppression, growing faint at the sight of violence; if that voice sounded not only in your brain, in your consciousness, but in the blood, in the nerves, and you in following it found yourself in real conflict with authority, spent part of your life in chains, or wandering in exile, and then suddenly the day for which you had waited half your life had dawned—then, like Mazzini, you would have spoken out in the square of Milan, spoken, in Italian, words of independence and brotherhood, to a thunder of applause, fearless of white uniforms and yellow moustachios; if, after ten years in prison, you, like Barbès, were carried by a exultant crowd on to the square of the very town where once an executioner's assistant had read your death sentence and another had pardoned you with life imprisonment, and then, after all this, found your ideal fulfilled and heard a crowd of two hundred thousand acclaim the martyr with the cry: "*Vive la République!*" and then, after that, had had to see Radetsky in Milan, Cavaignac in Paris, and again become a prisoner and an exile—imagine, besides, that you couldn't console yourself by laying all this at the door of brute force but, on the contrary, saw the people traitors to themselves, saw the same crowd now deliberating to whose hands to entrust the dagger turned against them—then you would not discuss so sensibly and so soundly whether thought is necessary and where the limits of freedom lie. No, you would have cursed these human herds, your love would have turned to hate; or, what is worse, to contempt. You might for all your atheism have gone into a monastery.'

'This would have been only proof that I am weak; confirmation that all men are weak, that thought is necessary not only for the world but even for man himself. But, forgive me, I simply cannot allow you to bring our conversation down to personalities. I will point out only one thing: yes, I am a spectator, but that is not my rôle and is not my nature. It is my condition. I have understood it, that is my happiness. Let's talk about my situation one day, but to-day I don't want to digress. You say that I would have cursed the people. Possibly; but that would have been very stupid. People, the masses, are elemental, they are oceanic, their path is the path of nature: they are her nearest heirs, they are led by dark instincts, unaccountable passions, they cling obstinately to what they have achieved, even if it is bad; hurled into motion, they sweep irresistibly with them or crush underfoot everything in their way, even if it is good. They march on like the famous Hindu idol. Everyone in the path of the idol throws himself under the chariot wheels, and it is often the most fanatical worshippers who are the first to be crushed. It is absurd to blame the people—they are right because they conform to the circumstances of their past life. They bear no responsibility for good or evil; they are facts, like good or bad harvests, like an oak tree, or a blade of grass. The responsibility lies more with the minority which represents the conscious thought of its age—though it too is not to blame. Altogether, the legal point of view is useless save in court, and that is why all the courts in the world are of no use at all. To understand and to blame is almost as absurd as not to understand and to execute. Is the minority to blame because all historical development, all the civilization of preceding days, was for its sake, that its mind has grown at the cost of the blood and the brain of others, that as a consequence of this it is far ahead of the brutalized, undeveloped masses, crushed by heavy toil? It is not a question of blame. It is one of the fatal, tragic aspects of history. The rich man is not responsible for the riches he finds in his cradle, nor the poor man for his poverty. They are both the victims of injustice, fatalism. And if we even have a certain right to demand that a suffering, oppressed and humiliated people, worn down with hunger and misery, should forgive us our unjust prerogatives, our superiority, our development, because we are not to blame for them, because we are striving to redress consciously our unconscious sin—where, then, shall we find the strength to curse and despise a people who have remained in the condition of Caspar Hauser [1] in order that you and I should read Dante and listen to Beethoven? To despise them because they do not understand us who enjoy a monopoly of understanding—is hideous, abominable cruelty. Remember how things were: the educated minority, having long enjoyed its privileged position, its aristocratic, literary, artistic, governmental ambience, at last felt a pang of conscience and remembered its forgotten brothers. The thought of the injustice of the social order, the thought of equality, flashed like an electric spark through the best minds of the last century. In a bookish, theoretical way, men realized the injustice of the times, and tried to redress it, bookishly. This tardy repentance on the part of the minority was called liberalism. In a genuine desire to reward the people for thousands of years of humiliation, they declared it sovereign, demanded that every peasant should suddenly become a political person, should grasp the complicated provisions of a half-free, half-servile code of law, abandon his work, that is, his daily bread, and that this new Cincinnatus should now concern himself with general issues. To the question of daily bread liberalism did not give much serious thought. It is too romantic to trouble itself with such gross requirements. It was easier for liberalism to invent the people than to study it. It told lies about it out of love, no less than others had out of hate. The liberals constructed their people *a priori*, created it out of memories of things read, dressed it up in a

[1]Caspar Hauser, mysterious youth supposed to have been the son of the Grand Duke of Baden, brought up in poverty owing to the machinations of the Grand Duchess, his step-mother.

Roman toga or a shepherd's cloak. No one thought about the real people. It lived, laboured, suffered nearby, round the corner, and if there was anyone who knew it, it was its enemies—the priests and the legitimists. Its lot remained unchanged, but the fictitious people became the idol of the new political religion. The holy oil with which the foreheads of the Tsars had been anointed, was transferred to its swarthy forehead covered with wrinkles and bitter sweat. Having freed neither its hands nor its mind, the liberals enthroned the people and, bowing down low before it, tried at the same time to retain power in their own hands. The people behaved like one of its representatives, Sancho Panza; it resigned the imaginary throne, or rather never sat on it. We are beginning to understand the falsehood on both sides. That means we are emerging on to the highway; let us point the way to everyone. But why should we start swearing when we look back on the past? Not only do I not blame the people, but I don't blame even the liberals. On the whole they loved the people after their own fashion. They sacrificed a great deal for their idea—that is always honourable—but they were on the wrong path. They may be compared to the early naturalists who began and ended their study of nature in the herbarium and the museum. All that they knew about life was the corpse, the dead form, the fossil of life. All honour to those who first thought of taking a knapsack and climbing mountains, sailing across seas, seizing on nature and life as they are. But why use their glory and successes to obscure the work of their predecessors? Liberals always lived in large towns and small circles. They were men of books, journals, clubs; they did not know the people at all; they studied it with immense profundity from historical sources, antiquities, not in the villages and the market place. We are all guilty of this to some degree, and hence misunderstandings, betrayed hopes, frustrations, and finally despair. If you were well acquainted with the inner life of France, you would not be surprised that the people want to vote for Bonaparte, and you would know that the French people have not the faintest notion of freedom, of the Republic, but they have bottomless national pride. They like Bonapartes and cannot bear the Bourbons without fully realizing why. The Bourbons remind them of the corvée, of the Bastille, of the nobility, whereas the Bonapartes recall old men's tales, the songs of Béranger, victories and, last but not least, the memory of how some neighbour of theirs—a peasant like themselves—returned a general, with the Legion of Honour on his chest. So the neighbour's son hurries off to vote for the nephew.'[1]

'Yes, of course, that is so. But one thing is strange—why, if their memory is so good, have they forgotten Napoleon's despotism, his conscriptions, the tyranny of the Prefets?'

'That is quite simple: for the people, despotism is not a peculiarity of the Empire. For it all governments so far have been despotic. For instance, it thinks of the republic, proclaimed for the pleasure of *La Réforme*, for the use of *Le National*—in terms of the 45 centimes tax, of deportations, of the poor workmen who weren't granted passes to Paris. The people, on the whole, are not good at philology. The word "republic" is nothing to them, they derive no comfort from it. Words like "Empire", "Napoleon", electrify them. That is enough for them.'

'If one looked at everything in this way, I should myself begin to think that not only would one never get angry or do anything, but one would lose all desire to do anything.'

'I thought I told you: to understand is already to act, to achieve. You think that when you have understood what is going on, your desire to act will pass? But that would mean that what you wanted to do was not what was wanted. In that case you must look out for some other work: if not outside, then within yourself. It's odd when man has something to do and does nothing, but it is no less odd when man has nothing to do and does it. Work is not at all like a

[1] Louis-Napoleon, later Napoleon III.

ball of wool which you give to a kitten to play with. It is determined not by desire alone, but also by the demand for it.'

'I have never doubted that one could always meditate, and I have never confused enforced inactivity with deliberate avoidance of thought. However, I foresee the comforting conclusion to which you will arrive: to remain in meditative idleness, paralysing the heart with the intellect and benevolence with criticism.'

'In order to participate actively in the world around us, I say again: love of humanity and mere wishes are not enough. All these are rather vague, flickering notions. What does it mean to love humanity? What is humanity itself? It all sounds to me like the old Christian virtues, *réchauffés* in a philosophical oven. People like their fellow citizens—that is understandable. But what the love is that embraces everything that has ceased to be a monkey, from the Eskimo and the Hottentot to the Dalai-Lama and the Pope—that I don't quite grasp, it's a little too wide. If it is the same love as that with which we love nature, the planets, the universe, I don't see how it could be particularly active: for it is only instinct, or understanding of the environment in which one lives, that can lead to action. Your instinct is gone: discard your abstract knowledge and face the truth like a hero, understand it and you will see what sort of action is needed and what isn't. Do you want political action within the present order? Then become a Marrast,[1] an Odilon Barrot[2] and you will have it. You don't want this, you feel that any decent man is outside all politics, that he can't seriously concern himself with such questions as

[1]Armand Marrast (1801–52). French Liberal statesman and publicist. Editor of *Le National*. Member of the Provisional Government and President of the National Assembly.

[2]Camille Hyacinthe Odilon Barrot (1791–1873), Liberal politician, opposed to Guizot. In 1848 tried with Thiers to form a ministry with Comte de Paris as Regent. President of Louis-Napoleon's first ministry, December 1848.

whether a republic needs or doesn't need a President, whether an Assembly may or may not send men to hard labour without trial, or, whether one should vote for Cavaignac or Louis Bonaparte? You may spend a month or a year thinking which of them is better; but you won't decide because they are, as children say, "both worse". All that is left for a self-respecting man is not to vote at all. Look at the other topics *à l'ordre du jour*, they are all the same, "consecrated to the gods"; death looms up behind them. What does a priest do when called in to attend a dying man? He doesn't try to cure him, he doesn't argue with his ravings; he reads the prayers for the dying. Follow his example, read the prayers, read the death sentence whose execution is a matter not of days but of hours, convince yourself once and for all that none of the condemned will escape death, neither the autocracy of the Petersburg Tsar, nor the *freedom* of the bourgois republic, and do not waste your pity on either. Better to persuade frivolous and superficial people who applaud the fall of the Austrian Empire and tremble for the fate of the demi-republic, that the fall of that republic is just as much of a step towards the liberation of peoples and thought as the fall of Austria, that there is no need for exceptions, for reprieves, that the time for clemency has not come; tell them in the words of liberal reactionaries that "amnesty is a thing of the future"; ask not for love of humanity, but for hatred of everything that hinders development, clutters the road, prevents progress. It is time to tie together with one rope all the enemies of development and freedom, just as they tie up their prisoners and parade them through the streets, so that everyone may see the joint responsibility of the French *code* and the Russian law, of Cavaignac and Radetsky. That will be a great lesson! He who is brought to his senses by these awful, momentous events, will never recover and will die like a Ritter von Toggenburg[1] of liberalism, like Lafayette.

[1] Swiss defender of obsolete rights.

The Terror executed men but our task is easier; we are called upon to execute institutions, destroy beliefs, break prejudices, shatter hopes of any return to the past, holding nothing sacred, making no concessions, showing no mercy. Our smile, our greetings are only for what is rising, for the dawn, and, if we are unable to bring it nearer, we can at least point out its approach to those who do not see it.'

'Like the old beggar in the Place Vendôme who offers his telescope every night to passers-by to look at the distant stars?'

'Your comparison is very apt; yes, point out to all passers-by how the waves of the chastising flood come closer and closer, how they swell and rise. At the same time, point out the white sail of the ark . . . far away, over there on the horizon. That's your work. When everything is engulfed, when everything superfluous has perished and dissolved in the salt water, when the waters begin to subside and the ark comes safely to rest, then men will have other things to do, many other things. But not now!'

PARIS, 1848
December 1st

V

CONSOLATIO

Der Mensch ist nicht geboren frey zu seyn.

GOETHE (*Tasso*

OF all the suburbs of Paris I like Montmorency best. There is nothing striking there, no carefully trimmed parks as at St. Cloud, no boudoirs of trees as at the Trianon. But one never wants to leave. In Montmorency nature is extremely simple. It is like the faces of certain women which do not strike, do not arrest us, but attract us by their sweet confiding expression, all the more because we are not aware of it. Such faces and landscapes usually have in them something at once touching and tranquil. It is for this tranquillity, for this drop of water to Lazarus, that the perpetually torn, agitated, agonized soul of modern man feels supremely thankful. On several occasions I have found peace in Montmorency, and for that I am grateful to it. There is a large grove there, situated high up, and quiet—to be found nowhere else near Paris. I do not know why, but this grove always reminds me of our Russian woods . . . one walks, and thinks that in a minute a whiff of smoke will drift across from the byres, in a moment the village will appear, there must be a manor-house on the other side; the road that goes there is wider and cuts through a clearing, and (can you believe it?) I then feel sad because a few moments later one comes out into the open and, instead of Zvenigorod, I see Paris and, instead of the small window of the priest's or farmer's cottage, I see the small window through which Jean-Jacques used to look out so long and so gloomily. . . .

To this very cottage, one day there approached from the grove, some people, apparently travellers. One was a lady about twenty-five years of age, dressed entirely in black, and the other a middle-aged man, prematurely grey. Their expression was serious, indeed grave and still. Only a long habit of concentration or a life rich in thoughts and events can lend this calm to the features. This calm is not natural, but the calm after storms, after struggle and victory.

'There is Rousseau's house,' said the man, pointing to the little building with no more than three windows.

They stopped. One window was slightly open, the curtain was moving in the wind.

'That movement of the curtain,' remarked the lady, 'frightens me—I cannot help it. I feel as if at any moment a suspicious, angry old man is going to pull it aside and ask us why we are standing here. Who, looking at this peaceful little house amongst the trees and shrubs, would imagine that it was the rock of Prometheus of a great man, whose only fault was that he loved men too much, believed in them too much, wished them more good than they wished themselves? His contemporaries could not forgive him for expressing their own secret remorse. They paid him back with forced contemptuous laughter and he resented it. They looked on the poet of liberty, of fraternity as a madman; they were afraid to recognize reason in him, for it would have meant admitting their own foolishness, and he wept for them. In a whole lifetime of devotion, of passionate desire to help, to love, to be loved, to liberate, he met with only a few passing salutations and endless coldness, arrogant incomprehension, persecution, slander. Nervous and tender by nature, he could not rise above these trifles and he wasted away, abandoned by everyone, in poverty and sickness. In answer to all his yearning for love and sympathy, he got only Thérèse. In her was concentrated for him everything that was warm, everything that was the heart: Thérèse, who never learnt to tell the time, and was an undeveloped being, full of prejudice, who reduced Rousseau's life to narrow suspiciousness, petty gossip, and in the end estranged him from his few remaining friends. How many bitter moments he must have spent leaning on this sill from which he fed the birds, wondering with what evil they would repay him! The only thing that remained for the poor old man was nature, and he delighted in it, and shut his eyes, eyes that were weary of life, heavy with tears. It was even said that he hastened on the moment of release. This time Socrates pronounced his own death sentence, for the sin of consciousness, for the crime of genius. When one seriously contemplates everything that is happening, one becomes disgusted with life. Everything in the world is nauseating, and stupid too; people run round in circles, work, don't find a moment's rest, and all produce absurdities. Others want to reason with them, to stop them, to save them, but are crucified and persecuted, and all this is done in a kind of delirium, without any effort to understand. The waters rise, race hard, whirl aimlessly, pointlessly. Here they break furiously against a rock, there they wash the shore. We stand in the middle of the whirlpool—there is nowhere to go. I know your view of life is different, doctor. Life does not irritate you, because you have only a physiological interest in it and ask little of it. You are a great optimist. Sometimes I agree with you—you confound me with your dialectic, but as soon as the heart enters the argument, as soon as one departs from generalities where everything is solved and at rest, and one touches upon living problems, perceives human beings, the soul rebels. Stifled for a moment, indignation mounts again, and one resents only one thing, that one hasn't sufficient power of hatred, of scorn for men for their indolent soullessness, their reluctance to rise higher, to be nobler. If only one could turn away from them, let them do what they wish in their cave, let them live to-day as they did yesterday, bolstered by custom and ritual, with blind beliefs about what is right and what is wrong . . . and moreover at every step betraying their own morality, their own catechism!'

'I don't think that you are fair. Are people to blame because you believe in them too much, because you have such an idealized opinion of their moral worth?'

'I can't understand what you're saying: I have just now said exactly the opposite. It doesn't seem to me to show an excessive belief in men to say of them that for every prophet they have only a martyr's crown and then vain remorse after his death, that they are ready to throw themselves, like beasts, at anyone who, acting as their conscience, calls their actions by their real names and who, accepting the burden of their sins, wants to awaken their consciousness.'

'Yes, but you forget the source of your indignation. You are angry with people for much that they haven't done, because you think them capable of all those admirable qualities for which you have educated yourself or have been educated; but they for the most part didn't have that education. I'm not angry, because I don't expect from people anything other than what they actually do. I see no reason or right to demand anything other than what they can give, and they can give only that which they do give. To ask for more, to accuse, is a mistake, is a resort to force. People are just only to madmen or total idiots; at least we don't accuse *them* of having badly constructed brains, we forgive them their natural defects, but on all others we make terrible moral demands. Why we should expect from every one we casually meet model virtues and unusual understanding, I do not know. Probably because of a tendency to idealize, to judge everything from above, just as life is commonly judged in terms of some dead letter, or passions in terms of some legal code, or individuals in terms of their lineage. I look at all this differently. I am accustomed to a doctor's point of view, which is totally contrary to that of a judge. A doctor lives in nature, in the world of facts and phenomena—he doesn't teach, he learns:

he seeks not revenge, but the alleviation of pain. When he sees suffering, when he sees defects, he looks for the reason, for the causal connexion; then he looks for remedies within this same world of facts. If there are none, he shrugs his shoulders sadly, is distressed by his ignorance, and doesn't think of punishment or retribution, and he doesn't condemn. The judge's view is simpler. In fact he doesn't need one at all—it is no accident that Themis is represented as blindfold. The less she sees of life, the juster she is. We poor doctors on the other hand would like even our fingers and ears to have eyes. I am neither a pessimist nor an optimist; I watch, I examine, without any preconceived notion, without any prepared ideals, and I am in no hurry to reach a verdict; I am merely—you must forgive me—more modest than you.'

'I don't know if I have understood you aright, but it seems to me that you find it natural that Rousseau's contemporaries should have tormented him with petty persecution, should have poisoned his life and slandered him; you forgive them their sins? That is very tolerant, but I don't know whether it is right or just.'

'In order to forgive sins one must first accuse. And I do not. But I may as well accept your expression. Yes, I forgive them the evil they have done as you forgive the cold weather that caused your child's illness the other day. Can one be angry with events that are independent of anyone's will, anyone's knowledge? Sometimes they can be very painful, but blame will not help: it will only confuse. When we sat by your child's bedside and her fever rose so high that even I was frightened, I felt bitter sorrow as I watched you and the sick child. You suffered so much in those hours; but instead of cursing the morbid condition of the blood and contemplating with hatred the laws of organic chemistry, I thought about something else, and that was how the capacity for understanding, feeling, love, affection, inevitably brings with it a corresponding capacity for misery, suffering, loss, moral resentment and bitterness. The tenderer the inner life, the harsher, the more destructive is the capricious game of chance which carries no responsibility for its actions.'

'But no, I didn't accuse the illness. Your simile doesn't quite fit for Nature has no consciousness at all.'

'And I think that one cannot be angry with the semi-conscious human mass. We must try and grasp its state of mind, its struggle between the premonition of light and the habits of darkness. You take as your standard, carefully grown, particularly successful hot-house flowers, which have had infinite care lavished on them, and you are angry because the wild ones are not as beautiful. Not only is that unjust, it is also very cruel. If the consciousness of the majority of people were more enlightened, can you possibly believe that they would live in the situation in which they do now? They harm not only others, but also themselves, and that is why they cannot be blamed. They are slaves to habit. They will die of thirst by the well, without suspecting that there is water in it, because their fathers never told them so. People have always been like this. It is time to give up being surprised or indignant; there has been time enough since Adam to get used to such things. This is the same romanticism that made poets angry because they have a body, because they feel hunger. You can be as angry as you like, but you will not change the world to fit a programme. It goes its own way; no one can deflect it from its course. Learn what its course is; and you will abandon your moralistic point of view and gain strength. Moral appraisal of events and the perpetual scolding of mankind belong to the most primitive stages of understanding. It may please one's vanity to distribute Montyon prizes[1] and preach homilies, taking oneself as the norm, but it is useless. There

[1] A philanthropist, Baron de Montyon (1733–1820) endowed prizes for virtue and literary distinction to be distributed by the Institut in Paris.

are people who have tried to apply this attitude to nature itself and have given various animals very good or very bad reputations. When they saw for instance that the hare runs away from obvious danger, they called him a coward. When they saw that the lion, who is twenty times bigger than a hare, doesn't run away from man and sometimes even eats him, they regarded him as brave. When they saw that a lion that is sated refuses to eat, they considered it magnanimity of spirit. A hare is as much a coward as a lion is generous or a donkey stupid. It is no longer possible to remain in the state of mind of Aesop's fables, one must envisage the world of nature and the world of man more simply, more calmly, more serenely. You speak about Rousseau's suffering. He was miserable, it is true, but it is also true that suffering always goes with exceptional development. A genius may sometimes not suffer if he withdraws into himself, satisfied by his own self, by art, by science, but in practical life this is not so. The matter is very simple: when such natures enter into ordinary human conditions, they upset the equilibrium, their surroundings are too narrow for them and are insupportable. They feel constructed by relations made for a different build, made to fit other shoulders which need them. Things that slightly irritate most men, that provoke mild argument and are put up with by ordinary people, develop into an intolerable pain in the breast of a strong man, flare up into furious protest, into open war, into a bold challenge to battle. This makes conflicts with one's contemporaries inevitable. The mob perceives scorn for what it holds dear, and flings mud and stones at the man of genius, until it understands that he was right. Is the genius to blame that he is above the crowd; is the crowd to blame that it does not understand him?'

'And you find this condition of people's minds—and what is more, that of a majority—normal, natural? According to you, this moral degradation, this stupidity, should go on like this?—You must be joking!'

'What else can one do? For no one forces them to behave like that. It is their own untutored will to do so. People, on the whole, lie less in practice than they do in words. The best proof of their simple-mindedness is their sincere readiness to repent as soon as they understand that they have committed a crime. Having crucified Christ, they suddenly realized they had behaved badly and threw themselves on their knees before the Cross. I cannot understand what moral degradation you have in mind, *si toutefois* you do not mean original sin. What was there to fall from? The further one looks back, the more one sees barbarism, lack of understanding, or else some totally alien line of development, which has almost no relation to us: perished civilization, Chinese manners. A long life in society develops the brain. This development is accomplished with difficulty, painfully. But instead of recognition of this fact, people are attacked for not being like the ideal sage invented by the Stoics or like the ideal saint invented by Christians. Whole generations have laid down their lives in order to make a small plot of earth habitable, centuries have been spent in struggle, blood has flowed in streams, generations have died in agonies, in vain efforts, in heavy labour, barely securing a precarious life and a little leisure, and the result was five or six brains who understood the rudiments of the social process and moved the masses towards the achievement of their destiny. The wonder is that men under these oppressive conditions ever arrived at their present moral state, at self-sacrifice, at patience, at a peaceful way of life; yes, we should wonder that men do so little evil, and not reproach them for not being each one of them an Aristides or a Simeon Stylites.'

'You wish to persuade me, doctor, that men are predestined to be rogues?'

'Believe me, men are pre-destined to nothing.'

'Then why do they live?'

'Just so, they are born and they live. Why does anything

live? This I think is the limit of all questions. Life—is both the means and the end, the cause and the effect. It is the eternal restlessness of active, tense matter striving for equilibrium only to lose it again, it is perpetual motion, the *ultima ratio*, beyond which one cannot go. In the past people used to look for answers in the clouds or in the depths, upwards or downwards, but they found nothing, because all that is essential, and important, is here on the surface. Life does not try to reach an aim, but realizes all that is possible, continues all that has been realized. It is always ready to go one step further in order to live more completely, to live more, if possible. There is no other aim. Very often we take as an aim what are the consecutive phases of some single development to which we have become accustomed. We believe that the aim of a child is its coming of age, because he does come of age; but the aim of a child is rather to play and enjoy himself, to be himself. If one looks for the final aim, then the purpose of everything living is—death.'

'You forget another aim, doctor, which is evolved by men but which survives them and is handed down from generation to generation, which grows from century to century. It is precisely in this life of the individual, inseparable from humanity, that there are revealed those constant aspirations towards which man advances, to which he rises and which one day he will realize.'

'I quite agree with you. I even said just now that the brain is being developed; the sum of ideas and their extent increases in conscious life, is handed down from generation to generation, but as to your last words permit me to express a doubt. Neither the aspiration, nor the correctness of it in any way guarantee its realization. Take the most universal, the most perpetual aspiration in all epochs and with all peoples: the aspiration to well-being, the aspiration that dwells in everything that feels the development of the usual instinct of self-preservation, the innate avoidance of everything that causes pain and the craving for everything that gives pleasure, the naive desire for things to be better, and not worse. Yet after thousands of years of work, humanity has not acquired even animal well-being. There is, I imagine, proportionately a greater amount of suffering amongst the slaves in Russia and of starvation amongst the Irish than amongst all the beasts and all the animals of the world. From this you can easily deduce how likely it is that other aspirations, less definite, and belonging to a minority, will be fulfilled.'

'Oh but surely the aspiration to freedom and independence is not inferior to hunger. It is not at all weak and is very definite.'

'That is not what history shows. It is true that some strata of society, developed under peculiarly fortunate circumstances, have certain tendencies towards freedom: but even so not very strong ones, if we are to judge by several thousands of years of slavery and by the present social order. Obviously, we are not speaking of exceptional natures for whom constraint is intolerable, but of the majority who give a constant *dementi* to these martyrs, a fact which caused the irritated Rousseau to utter his famous absurdity: "Man is born to be free—and is everywhere in chains!"'

'You repeat with irony this cry of indignation torn from the heart of a free man?'

'I see in it violation of history and contempt for facts. I find that intolerable. Such caprice offends me. Besides, it is a dangerous procedure to state *a priori*, as a fact, what is really the crux of the problem. What would you say to a man who, nodding his head sadly, remarked that "Fish are born to fly—but everywhere they swim"?'

'I should ask what makes him think that fish are born to fly.'

'Now you're becoming logical. But the ichthyophil is ready with his answer. First of all he will point out to you that the skeleton of a fish clearly shows a tendency to develop the extremities into legs and wings. He will then show you perfectly useless little bones that are a hint of the bone of a leg, or a wing. Then he will refer to flying fish, which prove, in fact, that *fishkind* not only aspires to fly, but also can do so on occasions. Having said all this in reply, he will be justified in asking you, in his turn, why you do not demand from Rousseau a justification for his statement that man must be free, seeing that he is always in chains. Why does everything else exist as it ought to exist, whereas with man, it is the opposite?'

'You are a most dangerous sophist, doctor, and if I did not know you so well, I should consider you most immoral. I do not know what superfluous bones there are in fishes. I know only that they have no lack of bones and I am convinced that men have a deep yearning for independence and for every kind of freedom. They stifle their inner voice with the futilities of life, and that is why I am angry with them. There is more comfort in my attacks on men than in your defence of them.'

'I knew that after exchanging a few words, we should then exchange roles, or better, that you would outflank me and emerge on the other side. You want to turn your back on people in indignation because they are incapable of attaining moral heights, independence, and all your ideals. At the same time, you look upon them as spoilt children. You are sure that they will soon improve and then be sensible. I know that people make haste very slowly. I have no confidence in their capacities, nor in those aspirations which are invented for them, and I put up with them as I do with these trees, these animals. I study them, even love them. Yours is an *a priori* point of view and you are perhaps logically right in saying that man should aspire to independence. I look at the question as a pathologist and see that up to now slavery has been the permanent condition of social development. Therefore either it is indispensable or it does not rouse as much disgust as it might seem to.'

'How is it that you and I, both examining history conscientiously see things so differently?'

'Because we are talking of different things. You, when speaking of history and nations, speak of flying fish, whereas I speak of fish in general. You contemplate the world of ideas divorced from facts, the line of thinkers and doers who represent the heights of consciousness in each epoch, the moments of energy when suddenly whole nations rise up and swallow at a single gulp a mass of ideas, in order to live them out quietly for centuries to come. You take these cataclysms which accompany the growth of nations, these exceptional individuals as routine events, but they are the climax, the limit of development. The existence of the educated minority who soar triumphantly above the heads of others and from century to century hand down their thoughts and aspirations which the masses, teeming below, have nothing to do with, is a shining testimony to how far human nature can develop, what a tremendous fund of strength exceptional circumstances can call forth; but all this has nothing to do with the masses, with mankind. The beauty of an Arab horse, bred over twenty generations, does not give us the slightest right to expect the same qualities in all horses. Idealists desperately desire to maintain their point at all costs. Physical beauty among human beings is as much the exception as uncommon ugliness. Look at the shopkeepers milling around in the Champs Élysées on a Sunday, or at the Epsom races, and you will be convinced that human nature is not at all beautiful.'

'I know this, and I am not at all surprised by the silly mouths, the greasy foreheads, the noses so impudently turned up or so absurdly drooping. I'm merely disgusted.'

'Yes, but think how you would laugh at a man who takes to heart the fact that cart horses are not as handsome as stags. For Rousseau the absurd social order of his time was intolerable; the small group of men who stood by his side and were educated to the point of lacking only the original genius to name the evil that oppressed them, responded to his call; these apostates, these nonconformists, remained faithful and formed "the Mountain" in '92. They nearly all perished, toiling for the French people, whose demands were very modest and who allowed them to be executed without compunction. I will not even call it ingratitude. Actually not everything these men did was done for the people. It is *ourselves* that we seek to set free, it is *we* who suffer from seeing the oppressed masses, *we* who are insulted by their slavery, *we* who suffer for them and want to end this suffering. What was there to be grateful for? Was the mob in the middle of the eighteenth century really able to desire freedom and the *Contrat Social*, when now, a century after Rousseau, half a century after the Convention, it is still blind to it, when, in the cramping framework of the most squalid form of social life, it gets on swimmingly like a fish in water?'

'The ferment of all Europe seems scarcely to bear out your point of view.'

'The dull ferment that agitates the peoples comes from hunger; if the proletarian were richer, he would never give a thought to communism. The bourgeois has enough to eat, his possessions are protected, so he has lost his interest in freedom, in independence; on the contrary, he now wants a strong government. When told indignantly that such-and-such a newspaper has been seized, that so-and-so is going to prison for his opinions, he only smiles. All this upsets and angers a small group of eccentric persons; the rest go their various ways unconcerned. They are busy, they buy and sell, they are family men. From this it does not in the least follow that we have no right to demand the fullest possible independence, but it does follow that we need not be angry with the people for being indifferent to our miseries.'

'That is so, but you seem to me to be a little too

arithmetical. It is a question not of counting heads, but of quality which gives moral force its *majority*.'[1]

'As to qualitative superiority, I concede it wholly to strong personalities. Aristotle for me represents not only the concentrated strength of his time but a great deal more. It took people two thousand years to understand him through and through, to grasp, at last, the meaning of his words. Do you remember, Aristotle calls Anaxagoras the first sober man among the drunken Greeks? Aristotle was the last. Put Socrates between the two and you have the complete list of sober men up to Bacon. It is hard to judge the masses by such exceptions.'

'Only the few have ever concerned themselves with knowledge; only exceptional, rigorous minds venture into this abstract field. If you do not find much sobriety among the masses, what you will find is an inspired intoxication, in which there is a vast wealth of sympathy for the truth. The masses did not understand Seneca or Cicero—but how they reacted to the call of the twelve apostles!'

'Do you know, sorry though one is for the apostles, one must admit, I think, that they were a complete *fiasco*.'

'Yes, they merely baptized half the universe.'

'In the course of four centuries of struggle, of six centuries of total barbarism. And after these efforts, lasting a thousand years, the world was baptized to such good effect that nothing was left of the apostolic teaching. The liberating spirit of the Gospel became tyrannical catholicism, the religion of love and equality a church of blood and war. The ancient world, its vital forces exhausted, was failing. Christianity arrived at its bedside as physician and consoler, but was infected itself by contact with the patient and became Roman, barbarian, anything you please, but not evangelistic. How great is the power of heredity, of the masses and circumstances! People think that it is enough to prove a truth as one would a mathematical theorem for it

[1] Augustine used the term *prioritas dignitatis*.—A.H.

to be accepted, that it is enough to believe oneself for others also to believe. What happens is quite different. Some say one thing, others listen to them and understand something quite different, because they have developed differently. What did the first Christians preach and what did the mob understand? The mob understood all that was unintelligible, all that was absurd and mystical; all that was clear and simple was beyond their grasp; the mob accepted everything that put chains on the conscience, nothing that liberated human beings. In the same way, later on, it understood the revolution only as bloody vengeance, guillotine, revenge. Bitter historical necessity became a cry of triumph. To the word "brotherhood" they stuck on the word "death"; "brotherhood or death" became a kind of "your money or your life" for the terrorists. We have lived through so much ourselves, seen so much, and our ancestors have lived so much of our lives for us, that it is surely unforgivable for us to lose our heads and imagine that it is enough to proclaim the Gospel to the Roman world to turn it into a democratic and social republic, as the *reds* used to think; or that it is enough to print two columns of an illustrated edition of the *Droits de l'homme* for man to become free.'

'Please tell me, why this passion for emphasizing only the worst side of human nature?'

'You started the conversation with a solemn curse against mankind and now you are defending it. You have just accused me of optimism, I return the charge. I have no system, no interest except the truth, and I express it as it appears to me. I do not deem it necessary out of politeness to humanity to attribute to it imaginary virtues and splendours. I hate phrases to which we have grown used, like Christians to the Creed. They may appear moral and good on the surface but they bind thought, they subjugate it. We accept them on trust and march on, leaving these treacherous beacons behind us, and lose our way. We become so used to them that we lose all capacity to doubt them and shrink from touching things so sacred. Have you ever considered the meaning of the words: "Man is born free"? I will translate them for you. They mean: "Man is born an animal"; no more. Take a herd of wild horses. There you have complete freedom and equal rights, perfect communism. But, on the other hand, development is impossible. Slavery is the first step towards civilization. In order to develop it is necessary that things should be much better for some and much worse for others; then those who are better off can develop at the expense of the others. In the cause of development nature spares nothing. Man is an animal with a remarkably well organized brain. Therein lies his power. He never knew in himself the tiger's litheness, nor the lion's strength. He did not have their wonderful sinews, nor the acuteness of their senses, but he discovered within himself infinite cunning and a multitude of tame qualities which, together with a natural inclination to live in herds, placed him on the first rung of social life. Do not forget that man loves to obey, always seeks to lean upon something, to hide behind something. He has not the proud self-reliance of the beast of prey. He grew up in subjection to the family and the tribe; the tighter and more complex the knot of social life, the deeper the servitude into which men fell. They were crushed by religion, which oppressed them for their cowardice, by elders who oppressed them in the name of tradition. No animal, except the breeds "corrupted by man", as Byron called domestic animals, would have survived these human relations. The wolf eats the lamb because it is hungry and because the lamb is weaker, but the wolf doesn't demand slavery from the lamb, the lamb doesn't submit; it protests with cries, with flight; man introduces into the animal world of savage independence and self-assertion an element of loyal and humble service, the element of Caliban. That alone made possible the development of Prospero. And here again is the same merciless economy of nature, her calculation of means, whereby an excess in one direction is paid for by unfulfillment in another, so that, having stretched the neck and front legs of the giraffe to fantastic lengths, she stunts its hind legs.'

'Why, doctor, you are a dreadful aristocrat!'

'I am a naturalist, and do you know what else? . . . I am not a coward, I am not afraid of learning the truth, nor of expressing it.'

'I shall not argue against you. In any case, in theory, everyone speaks the truth so far as he understands it—there is not much courage in that.'

'You think so? What a prejudice! . . . Why, out of a hundred philosophers you will not find one who is candid. One would not mind what mistakes they made, what nonsense they talked, if only they were completely sincere. Some deceive others from moral motives, others deceive themselves for the sake of peace. Will you find many like Spinoza or Hume who fearlessly go where the truth leads them? All these great liberators of the human mind behaved like Luther and Calvin, and may have been right from a practical point of view. They liberated themselves and others until they came up against some form of slavery, symbolic book, holy writ, and then found enough restraint and moderation in their souls not to go further. Most of their followers continue to walk strictly in the steps of their masters; among them there appear now and again men slightly bolder than the rest who begin to suspect that matters are not quite so simple, but keep silent out of piety and lie out of respect for the subject, like lawyers, who every day affirm that they cannot doubt the impartiality of the judges, knowing perfectly well that they are crooks whom they don't begin to trust. This courtesy is purely servile but we have got used to it. It is not easy to know the truth, but even that is easier than to express it when it does not tally with public opinion. What finessing, what rhetoric, what circumlocution, what sugaring of the pill the best minds like Bacon or Hegel resorted to in order to avoid plain speaking, for fear of stupid indignation or vulgar catcalls! That is why it is so difficult to understand science—one has to guess at the truth through its false garb. And now judge for yourself whether there are many who have the desire and leisure to delve down to the inner thought and rummage around in the manure with which our teachers cover over their fettered understanding, and tear away the fake diamonds and the painted glass of their science.'

'This again is close to your aristocratic idea that truth is only for the few and falsehood is for all, that . . .'

'Allow me, this is the second time that you have called me an aristocrat; which reminds me of Robespierre's remark: "*l'athéisme est aristocrate.*" If all Robespierre wanted to say was that atheism is open only to the few, in the same way as the differential calculus, or physics, he would have been right, but when he said: "Atheism is aristocratic", he concluded from this that atheism was false. I find this disgusting, this is demagogy, the submission of reason to an absurd majority vote. The inflexible logician of the revolution faltered, and in declaring a *democratic* untruth did not thereby restore popular religion but only showed the limits of his power, showed the frontier beyond which even he was not a revolutionary; and to show this in the hour of revolution and movement is to bring home to one that the hour of the individual has passed . . . And in fact after the Fête de l'Être Suprême Robespierre becomes gloomy, preoccupied, anxious; he is plunged in melancholy. Gone are his earlier faith and the bold step with which he walked, with which he passed through blood and was not defiled; then he knew no frontiers, the future had no bounds. Now he sees the wall, feels that he has to be conservative, and the head of the atheist Cloots, sacrificed to prejudice, lies at his feet, like proof of guilt which he cannot step over. We are older than our elder brothers. Let us not be children.

Let us not shrink either from reality or logic, or reject the consequences. They are beyond our power. Do not let us invent God. If He does not exist, this will not make Him exist the more. I said that truth belongs to the minority. Did you not know this? Why did it seem strange to you? Because I did not use a rhetorical phrase? But, let me assure you, I am not responsible either for the good or bad consequences of this fact. I merely speak of its existence. In the present as in the past, I see knowledge, truth, moral strength, craving for independence, love of beauty, in a small group of men, antagonistic, unsympathetic to the majority, lost in their milieu. On the other side, I see the painful advance of the other strata of society, narrow ideas based on tradition, mean needs, petty efforts towards good, petty tendencies towards evil.'

'And, you must add, an extraordinary soundness in their aspirations.'

'You are right. The general sympathies of the masses are usually sound like the instincts of animals, and do you know why? Because the pitiable independence of separate individuals is obliterated in the social mass. The merit of the masses lies in their impersonality, whereas the development of the independent personality constitutes that excellence which everything that is free, gifted and strong is striving to achieve.'

'Yes . . . so long as there is such a thing as the masses. But note that the past and the present give you no reason to conclude that these conditions will not change in the future. Everything is leading towards the destruction of the decrepit foundations of social life. You have seen clearly and described pungently the duality, the conflict of life; and on this you rest. Like the Public Attorney in a criminal court, you state the crime and try to prove it, and then leave the verdict to the tribunal. Others go further—they want to eradicate the crime. All the strong natures among the minority of which you speak have always striven to fill the chasm separating them from the masses. The thought that this was an inexorable, fatal fact was hateful to them. They had too much love in their hearts to remain upon their isolated eminence. With the passionate recklessness of a generous impulse they preferred to perish in the chasm that separated them from the people, rather than stroll along the edge as you do. And this tie of theirs with the masses is not a whim, not rhetoric, but the deep feeling of kinship, the consciousness that it is from the masses that they themselves have emerged, that without this chorus they would not themselves exist, that they represent its aspirations, that they have achieved what it is in the course of achieving.'

'No doubt every full-blown talent is joined like a flower, to the plant by a thousand threads and could not exist without a stem, but all the same it is not itself a stem, nor a leaf, but a flower. Its life, united as it is with the other parts, is nevertheless other. One cold dawn—and the flower perishes, but the stem will remain. The flower, if you like, is the aim of the plant and the limit of its life, but nevertheless the petals of the corolla are not the whole plant. Every epoch, so to say, spills out a rolling wave of its fullest and best organisms, provided that they have found the means to develop. Not only do they leave the crowd, they *come out* of it. Take Goethe; he represents the concentrated, intensified, distilled, chemically *sublimated* essence of Germany. He came out of it, and could not have existed without the whole history of his people, but he drew so far away from his compatriots into the sphere into which he rose, that they could not understand him well, and he, too, in the end, understood them badly. In him was gathered up everything that moved the soul of the protestant world and unfolded in such a way that he soared over the world of his day like the spirit of God upon the face of the waters. Below was chaos, misunderstanding, scholasticism, painful efforts to understand. In him there was luminous awareness and tranquil thought, far in advance of his contemporaries.'

'Goethe represents your very thought with particular splendour, he withdraws, he is content with his greatness; in this respect he is an exception. Not so were Schiller and Fichte, Rousseau and Byron, and all those who struggled painfully to raise the masses, the crowd, to their level. I prefer the torments of these men, hopeless, consuming, often following them to the grave, sometimes to the scaffold or the madhouse, to Goethe's peace.'

'They suffered a great deal, but do not think they were without consolation. They had much love and still more faith. They believed in humanity as they had invented it, they believed in the future, while indulging in despair, and this faith strengthened their exaltation.'

'And why have you no faith?'

'Byron answered that question long ago. He replied to a lady who was trying to convert him to the Christian faith: "What should I do to begin to believe?" In our times, one can either believe without thinking or think without believing. You think that doubt, calm on the surface, is easy, but can you know what a man, in a moment of pain, weakness, exhaustion, might not be ready to give for a belief? But where will you acquire it? You say that it is better to suffer and you advise me to have faith, but do religious people really suffer? I shall tell you an incident which happened to me in Germany. I was called to an hotel to see a foreign lady who had just arrived, and whose children had fallen ill; I went; the children were in the throes of appalling scarlet fever. Medicine has made such progress in our day that we now realize that we understand scarcely any illness or any treatment; that is a great step forward. I saw that things were very bad. To calm the mother I prescribed several innocuous things, gave instructions, somewhat fussy ones, in order to occupy her, and then settled down to wait and see what strength the body would find to fight the disease. The elder boy became quite still. "He seems to have peacefully fallen asleep," his mother said to me. I made a sign to her not to disturb him. The boy was dying. It was clear to me that the disease would take the same course with the other child. It seemed to me impossible to save her. The mother, a very nervous woman, was out of her mind and prayed without ceasing. The girl died. During the first days nature won—the mother lay in a fever, was on the edge of death herself, but little by little her strength returned. She became quieter, kept talking to me, always about Swedenborg. When she went away, she took me by the hand and said with an air of quiet triumph: "It was hard for me. . . . It was a terrible trial! . . . But I placed them well, they went back pure, not a speck of dust, not one corrupting breath ever touched them. . . . They will be happy! For their good I must submit!" '

'What a difference between such fanaticism and man's faith in humanity, faith in the possibility of a better order, of freedom. That is knowledge, thought, conviction, not superstition.'

'Yes. That is thought, logic, abstraction and for that reason is not the gross religion *des Jenseits*, which places children *en pension* in the other world, but the religion *des Diesseits*, the religion of science, of universal, hereditary, transcendental reason, of idealism. Could you please explain to me why belief in God is ridiculous and belief in humanity is not; why belief in the kingdom of heaven is silly, but belief in utopias on earth is clever? Having discarded positive religion, we have retained all the habits of religion, and having lost paradise in heaven we believe in the coming paradise on earth, and boast about it. Faith in life after death gave so much strength to the martyrs of the early centuries, but then the very same faith supported the martyrs of the revolution. Both so proudly and gaily took their heads to the block, because they had an unquenchable faith in the success of their ideas, in the triumph of Christianity or the triumph of the republic. Both were mistaken—the martyrs were not resurrected, the republic was not established. We came after them and witnessed it. I do not deny grandeur or utility to faith—it is the great source of movement, of advance, of passion in history, but faith in the human soul is either an individual matter or an epidemic. You cannot conjure it up, particularly not with someone who has allowed himself to analyse, to doubt, to be sceptical, who has tested life and, with bated breath, has looked on, enrapt, at every anatomical dissection, who has peered behind the scenes more perhaps than was necessary. The deed is done, one can't believe again. How, for instance, can I be convinced that the soul of man lives on after death when it is so easy to see the absurdity of this division between body and soul? How can I be convinced that to-morrow or next year social brotherhood will come about, when what I see is that people understand brotherhood in the spirit of Cain and Abel?'

'For you, doctor, there remains a humble *a parte* in this tragedy. Sterile criticism and idleness to the end of your days.'

'It may be, it may well be. Though I do not consider inner activity idleness. I believe, nevertheless, that you judge my fate correctly. Do you remember the Roman philosophers in the first centuries of Christianity? Their position had much in common with ours; the present and the future had slipped away from them, they were on bad terms with the past. Convinced that they had a better and clearer understanding of the truth they looked on sorrowfully at the world that was being destroyed and the world that was being created. They felt themselves to be more right than either and weaker than both. Their circle became smaller and smaller. They had nothing in common with paganism except habit and way of life. The contrivances of Julian the Apostate and his restoration were just as ridiculous as the restoration of Louis XVIII and Charles X. On the other hand, the Christian theodicy insulted their worldly wisdom; they could not accept its language; the earth vanished from under their feet, sympathy for them evaporated, but they knew how to wait, proudly and grandly, until destruction overtook now one, now another. They knew how to die, not courting death and without any claims to save themselves or the world, they died calmly and with indifference to their fate. If death spared them, they knew how to wrap themselves in their togas and silently observe what happened to Rome, to humanity. The one blessing that remained for these people who were strangers to their own times, was a quiet conscience, the consoling knowledge that they had not been afraid of the truth, that having once grasped it they had found the strength to endure it and to remain faithful to it.'

'And no more than that?'

'As though that wasn't enough? Although, no, I have forgotten yet another blessing: their personal relations, the certainty that there were others who also understood, who sympathized with them, the certainty of a profound *rapport* that was independent of events; and if you add a little sun, the sea in the distance, or mountains, rustling trees, a warm climate . . . What more can one want?'

'Unfortunately such a peaceful corner with its warmth and quiet is now nowhere to be found in Europe.'

'I shall go to America.'

'It is very boring there.'

'That's true. . . .'

PARIS, 1849
March 1st

VI

OMNIA MEA MECUM PORTO

Ce n'est pas Catilina qui est à vos portes—c'est la mort!
PROUDHON (*Voix du Peuple*)

Komm her, wir setzen uns zu Tisch!
Wen sollte solche Narrheit ruehren?
Die Welt geht auseinander wie ein fauler Fisch
Wir wollen sie nicht balsamiren.
GOETHE

THE old, official Europe that one can see is not asleep—it is dying!

The last frail and sickly vestiges of its former life are scarcely sufficient to hold together for a time the disintegrating parts of its body which are striving to combine afresh and to enter into new forms.

At first sight, there is much that is still normal; things run smoothly, judges judge, the churches are open, the stock exchange hums with activity, armies manoeuvre, palaces blaze with light, but the soul of life has fled, everyone is uneasy at heart, death is at our elbow, and, in reality, nothing goes well. In reality there is no church, no army, no government, no judiciary. Everything has become the police. The police is guarding and saving Europe, under its protection stand thrones and altar. It is the galvanic current by which life is being unnaturally kept going in order to gain the present moment. But the consuming fire of the disease is not extinguished, it has only been driven inward, it has been concealed. All those blackened walls and monuments which seem to have acquired with age the everlasting quality of rocks—are insecure. They are like the tree-stumps that remain long after the forest has been felled. They preserve a look of stubborn indestructibility, until someone gives them a kick.

Many do not see death, only because by death they imagine some kind of annihilation. Death does not annihilate the constituent parts, but loosens them from their former whole, gives them the freedom to exist under other conditions. Obviously a whole part of the world cannot disappear from the face of the earth. It will remain just as Rome remained in the Middle Ages; it will dissolve, merge into the coming Europe and lose its present character, at once submitting to and influencing the new. An inheritance left by a father to a son prolongs, physiologically and socially, the life of the father beyond the grave; nevertheless, between the two of them there is *death*—just as between the Rome of Julius Caesar and the Rome of Gregory VII.[1]

The death of the contemporary forms of social order ought to gladden rather than trouble the soul. But what is frightening is that the departing world leaves behind it not an heir, but a pregnant widow. Between the death of one and the birth of the other much water will flow by, a long night of chaos and desolation will pass.

We shall not live to see what Simeon the receiver of God lived to see. Hard as this truth may be, we must make our peace with it, accept it, for it is impossible to alter.

For some time we have been studying the sickly organism of Europe on all its levels; always we have discovered nearby the stamp of death and only rarely in the distance heard prophecy. We, too, at first hoped, believed, tried to believe. The death agony distorted one feature after another so

[1]On the other hand, between the Europe of Gregory VII, of Martin Luther, of the Convention, of Napoleon, there is not death but development, transformation, growth; that is why all the efforts of ancient reactionary movements (Rienzi, Brancaleone) were impossible, while monarchic restorations in the new Europe are so easy.—A.H.

rapidly that it became impossible for us to deceive ourselves. Life was going out like the last candles in windows before the dawn. We were appalled, frightened. With hands folded we watched the terrible progress of death. What have we seen since the February revolution? All we can say is that two years ago we were young, and now we are old.

The closer we came to the parties and the people, the vaster became the desert around us, the vaster grew our loneliness. How was one to share the insanity of the former, the soullessness of the latter? On the one side, sloth, apathy; on the other, lies and narrow-mindedness: strength and energy, nowhere; save for a few martyrs who died for the people without bringing them any benefit, a few sufferers ready to crucify themselves for the crowd, ready to give their blood, their heads, but, seeing that the masses did not need these sacrifices, compelled to keep both.

Lost without occupation in this world, deafened by senseless quarrels, daily insults, we surrendered to grief and despair, and wished only for one thing—to find somewhere to rest our tired heads, without caring whether or not we should dream.

But life claimed her due, and instead of despair, instead of the desire to perish, I now want to live. I no longer want to admit to such dependence on the world. Nor do I want to remain for the rest of my life at the bedside of the dying like an eternal mourner.

Is it possible that there is nothing in us at all, and that it is only because of, and within, this world that we were something—so that, now that it is dying, undermined by other laws, we have nothing to do but to sit mournfully on its ruins, no other calling but to serve as its tombstone?

Enough mourning. We have given back to the world that which belonged to it. We did not spare ourselves, we gave it the best years of our lives and the full sympathy of our hearts; we suffered its suffering more than it did itself. Now let us dry our eyes and look manfully around us. We can, *we must* find the strength to bear whatever lies ahead. We have lived through the worst, and a misfortune lived through is a misfortune past. We have had time to acquaint ourselves with our situation. We have no hopes, we expect nothing, or, rather, we expect everything; it comes to the same. There is much that can humiliate us, break us, kill us—but *nothing* can surprise us . . . or else all our thoughts and words have been but on our lips.

The ship is sinking. Terrible was the moment of doubt when there was hope as well as danger. Now the situation is clear, the ship cannot be saved. All that is left is to perish or save oneself. Abandon ship! To the boats! Cling to the wreckage! Let everyone try his luck, test his strength. The *point d'honneur* of sailors is not for us.

Out of the oppressive room where a long, stormy life is ending! Come out into the fresh air away from the heavy, infectious atmosphere, out into the fields from the sickroom! Many masters will be found to embalm the corpse, and yet more worms to feast on the rotting body. Let us leave the corpse to them, not because they are better or worse than us, but because they want it and we do not, because they thrive on it and we suffer. Let us stand aside, free and detached, knowing that we have no inheritance and no need of one.

In the old years, such an arrogant break with the present would have been called *escape*. Incurable romantics will call it that even to-day after all the events that have taken place before their eyes.

But a free man cannot run away, because he depends solely on his convictions and on nothing else. He has the right to go or to remain. The question is not one of escape, but whether man is free or not.

Moreover, the word *escape* becomes inexpressibly ludicrous when applied to those who had the misfortune to see further, to go further than the others could, and now do not wish to return. They could have said to the others, as

Coriolanus did, 'It is not we who run, but you who remain behind,' but both are absurd. We do what we can, those around us do what they can. The development of the individual and of the masses is such that they cannot take complete responsibility for consequences. But a certain stage of development, however it happened or was brought about, brings some obligations. To abjure one's development is to abjure oneself.

Man is freer than is usually believed.

He depends a great deal on his environment, but not as much as he surrenders to it. A large part of our destiny lies in our hands. One should grasp it and not let it go. But understand this, people allow the external world to overcome them, to captivate them against their will; they renounce their independence, depending on all occasions not on themselves but on the world, pulling ever tighter the knots that bind them to it. They expect from the world all the good and evil in life, the last thing they rely on is themselves. With such childish submission, the fatal power of the external becomes invincible; to enter into battle with it seems madness. Yet this terrible power wanes from the moment when in a man's soul, instead of self-sacrifice and despair, instead of fear and submission, there arises the simple question: 'Am I really so fettered to my environment in life and death that I have no possibility of freeing myself from it even when I have in fact lost all touch with it, when I want nothing from it and am indifferent to its bounty?'

I am not saying that this protest in the name of the independence and self-reliance of the individual is easy. It is not freely torn from the breast of man; either long, personal trials and misfortunes precede it, or else, those hard times when the more man understands the world, the more he is at odds with it, when all the bonds that link him to the external world have become chains, when he feels that he is right in despite of events and the masses, when he realizes that he is an enemy, a stranger, and not a member of a large family to which he belongs.

Outside us everything changes, everything vacillates. We are standing on the edge of a precipice and we see it crumbling. Twilight descends and no guiding star appears in the sky. We shall find no haven but in ourselves, in the consciousness of our unlimited freedom, of our autocratic independence. Saving ourselves in such a fashion, we take our stand on that open, manly ground which alone makes possible the development of a free existence in society—if it is at all possible for humanity.

If only people wanted to save themselves instead of saving the world, to liberate themselves instead of liberating humanity, how much they would do for the salvation of the world and the liberation of humanity!

The dependence of man on his environment and his epoch is indubitable. It is all the stronger for half the ties being fastened outside his consciousness. There is the physiological tie against which the will and the brain can rarely struggle; there is the hereditary element which comes to us, like our facial features, at birth, and which constitutes the link between the present generation and all those that have gone before; then there is the physiologico-moral element, education, which grafts man on to history and the present day. Finally, there is the conscious element. The environment into which a man is born, the epoch in which he lives lead him to participate in whatever is happening around him, to continue what was begun by his fathers; it is natural that he should become attached to that which surrounds him, for he cannot but reflect in and through himself his times and his environment.

But it is precisely in the form of the reflexion that his independence manifests itself. The reaction provoked in man by his environment is the response of his personality to the influence of the milieu. This response can be full of understanding as well as full of contradiction. The moral independence of man is just as irrefutably true and real as his dependence on his milieu, with this difference—that one is in inverse relation to the other. The greater the awareness, the greater the independence; the weaker the awareness, the stronger the ties with the environment, the more does the environment absorb the individual. In this way, instinct without awareness does not reach true independence, and then man's self-reliance manifests itself either as the wild freedom of an animal, or in those rare, spasmodic and inconsistent denials of this or that aspect of society which are called crimes.

The awareness of independence does not necessarily imply a break with the milieu. Self-reliance does not necessarily involve hostility to society. The milieu does not always stand in the same relation to the world, and consequently does not always provoke resistance on the part of the individual.

There are periods when man is free *in a common cause.* Then the activity towards which every energetic nature strives, coincides with the aspirations of the society in which he lives. At such times—which are rare enough—everything flings itself into the whirlpool of events, in it finds life, joy, suffering and death. Only natures of unique genius, like Goethe, stand aside, while natures that are colourless and common remain indifferent. Even those who fight against the main stream are also carried away and find satisfaction in the real struggle. The emigrés were just as absorbed by the Revolution as the Jacobins. In such times there is no need to talk of self-sacrifice and devotion. They appear of their own accord and very easily. None retreat because all believe. There are, ultimately, no sacrifices. What seem like sacrifices to onlookers are actions that are simple fulfilment of desires, a natural mode of behaviour.

There are other periods—and they are the most frequent of all—peaceful, even sleepy periods, when the relations of man to his milieu *persist* as they were left by the last upheaval. They are not so taut as to snap, not so oppressive as to become unbearable, and finally not so extraordinary or exacting as to prevent life from making good the main defects and smoothing over the roughest edges. In such periods the problem of the connexion between society and the individual does not occupy the mind so much. Private conflicts, tragic disasters occur destroying a few individuals; the titanic groans of the man in chains can be heard, but all this is swallowed up without a trace in the established order; recognized relations remain unshaken, resting as they do on habit, on human fecklessness, on indolence, on the lack of the demonic element of criticism and irony. People are absorbed in personal concerns, in family life, in learning and industry, they propose and dispose, imagining that they are getting things done. They work hard to arrange the future of their children; their children, in their turn, arrange the lives of their children, so that the existing individuals, the whole of the present, as it were efface themselves, regarding themselves as something transient. Such a situation survives to this very day in China and to some extent in England.

But there are periods of a third kind, very rare and the saddest of all—periods when the forms of social life, having outlived themselves, slowly and painfully perish. The civilization of the élite not only reaches its peak, but transcends the sphere of possibilities vouchsafed by historical conditions, so that it seems to belong to the future; but actually it is divorced in equal measure from the past which it despises and from the future which develops according to other laws. This is the moment when the individual comes into conflict with society. The past figures as a kind of frantic resistance. Violence, lies, cruelty, corrupt servility, narrowness, the loss of all sense of human dignity, become the general rule of the majority. All that was heroic in the past has by now gone. The decrepit world has no longer any belief in itself and defends itself desperately because it is frightened. In its desire for self-preservation it forgets its gods, tramples on rights by which it lived, repudiates culture and honour, becomes bestial, persecutes, kills, but all the while power remains in its hands. It is obeyed not out of cowardice alone, but because on the other side all is uncertain, nothing decided, nothing ready—above all men are not ready. On this other side, the unknown future looms up on a horizon wrapped in cloud, a future that confounds all human logic. The issue of the Roman world was decided by Christianity, a religion with which the free man of declining Rome had as little in common as he had with polytheism. Humanity, in order to move forward and emerge from the narrow limits of Roman law, retreated into German barbarism.

Those among the Romans who, from the tedium of life, pursued by despair and fear, threw themselves into Christianity, were saved. But those who suffered no less, but possessed stronger characters and intellect and had no desire to be saved from one absurdity by another—are they deserving of blame? Could they stand for the old gods with Julian the Apostate or for the new with Constantine? Could they take part in the cause of the day, seeing where the spirit of the times was taking them? In such periods it is easier for a free man to become a savage in isolation from his fellow-men, than to march along the same road with them, easier to take his own life than to sacrifice it.

Is a man less right merely because no one agrees with him? Does the mind stand in need of any other warrant than that of the mind? And how can universal insanity refute personal conviction?

The wisest of the Romans vanished from the scene completely, and did well to do so. They scattered along the shores of the Mediterranean Sea, disappeared for the others in the silent grandeur of their grief—but for themselves they did not disappear. And fifteen centuries later we must admit that they in fact were the conquerors, they the sole, the free, the powerful representatives of the independent human personality and dignity. They were men, they could not be counted like heads of cattle, they did not belong to the herd, and not wishing to lie, and having nothing in common with the herd—they withdrew.

And what have we in common with the world around us? A few individuals who share our convictions; the three just men of Sodom and Gomorrah, they are in the same position as we; they represented the protesting minority, strong in thought, weak in action. Apart from them, we have no more real link with the modern world than we have with China (for the moment I waive all physiological links and habits). This is so true that even on those rare occasions when people utter the same words as we do, they understand them differently. Do you want the *liberty* of the Mountain, the *order* of the Legislative Assembly, the slave labours of Egypt offered by the Communists?

Everyone now plays with his cards on the table, and the game itself has become greatly simplified, it is impossible to make mistakes: in every corner of Europe there is the same struggle, the same two camps. You feel quite clearly which you are against, but do you feel your tie with the other camp as clearly as your hatred and disgust for that of the enemy?

The time for frankness has come. Free men do not deceive either themselves or others; every reprieve leads to something false and devious.

The year which has passed, to end worthily, to fill the cup of moral degradation and torment, offered us a terrible spectacle: the fight of *a free man against the liberators of humanity*. The bold words, the mordant scepticism, the fierce denial, the merciless irony of Proudhon angered the official revolutionaries no less than the conservatives. They attacked him bitterly, they defended their traditions with the inflexibility of legitimists, they were terrified of his atheism and his anarchism, they could not understand how one could be free without a state, without a democratic government. In amazement they listened to the immoral statement that the republic is for man, not man for the republic. And when logic and eloquence failed them, they declared Proudhon a suspect, they placed him under a revolutionary anathema, expelling him from their communion of true believers. The talent of Proudhon and the bestiality of the police saved him from calumny. The dastardly charge of treason was passing from mouth to mouth among the democratic rabble, when he hurled his famous articles at the President who, deafened by the blow, could not find a better answer than to persecute the convict imprisoned for his ideas and words. Seeing this, the mob grew calmer.

And these are the crusaders of freedom, the privileged liberators of humanity! They are frightened of freedom, they need a master to prevent them from becoming spoilt, they need authority because they do not trust themselves. Is it surprising after this to find that the handful of people who migrated with Cabet to America had barely settled down in the makeshift huts when all the objectionable elements of European political life revealed themselves in their midst?

With all that, *they* are more modern than we, more useful, because closer to reality. They will find more sympathy among the masses, they are more needed. The masses want to stay the hand that impudently snatches from them the bread they have earned—that is their fundamental desire. They are indifferent to individual freedom, to freedom of speech; the masses love authority. They are still dazzled by the arrogant glitter of power, they are affronted by the sight of someone who stands apart. By equality, they understand equality of oppression; afraid of monopolies and privileges, they look askance at talent and allow no one not to do what they do. The masses want a social government that would govern *for* them, and not like this existing one, *against* them. To govern themselves doesn't enter their heads. That is why the *liberators* are much closer to the present revolutions than any *free man* could be. A free man may be totally useless, but it does not follow from this that he should act against his convictions.

But, you may say, one must be moderate. I doubt whether anything would come of it. Even when a man gives himself up completely to a task, he does not achieve much. What then will he achieve if he deliberately deprives himself of half his strength and organs? Make Proudhon a Minister of Finance, a President—he will become a sort of inverted Bonaparte. Bonaparte is in a perpetual state of vacillation, indecision, because he is obsessed by the idea of being Emperor. Proudhon would also be in a constant state of bewilderment, because the existing republic is just as detestable to him as it is to Bonaparte, and at present a social republic is much less likely than an empire.

However, as for the man who still can or wants to take part in party struggles, although he is aware of inner disharmony, he who feels no urge to go his own way although he sees that the way of others is not right, he who does not think that it is better to lose one's way, to perish altogether, than surrender what he knows to be true—let him work with the others. He will even do good perhaps because, whatever else, these liberators of humanity will drag down with them into the abyss the ancient forms of monarchist Europe. I acknowledge the rights of those who wish to act as fully as the rights of those who wish to withdraw. That is their affair, and we are not discussing this topic.

I am very glad to have touched upon this obscure question, this strongest of all the chains by which man is fettered; the strongest, because either he does not feel the violence it does to him or, what is worse, he considers it to be absolutely just. Let us see if this chain, too, has not grown rusty.

The submission of the individual to society, to the people,

to humanity, to the Idea, is merely a continuation of human sacrifice, of the immolation of the lamb to pacify God, of the crucifixion of the innocent for the sake of the guilty. All religions have based morality on obedience, that is to say, on voluntary slavery. That is why they have always been more pernicious than any political organization. For the latter makes use of violence, the former—of the corruption of the will. Obedience means the transference of all that is most individual in a man on to an impersonal, generalized sphere independent of him. Christianity, the religion of contradictions, recognized on the one hand the infinite worth of the individual, as if only for the purpose of destroying him all the more solemnly before Redemption, the church, the Father in Heaven! These notions impregnated the whole of social life, were elaborated into a complete system of moral subjection, into a perverted but completely consistent dialectic. The world becoming more worldly or, better, noticing at last that it was actually just as worldly as ever, introduced its own elements into the Christian moral doctrine, but the foundation remained the same. The individual, who is the true, real monad of society, has always been sacrificed to some social concept, some collective noun, some banner or other. For whose sake this was done, to whom the sacrifice was made, who profited by it, who was liberated at the price of the individual's freedom, no one ever asked. Everyone sacrificed (at least in words) himself and everyone else.

This is not the place to examine how far the backwardness of the people justified such educational measures. Probably these measures were natural and indispensable, we come across them everywhere, but we can boldly say that even if they achieved large results, they certainly retarded the course of development, at least as much, distorting the mind with a false vision. On the whole I believe very little in the utility of lies, particularly if they are no longer believed in: all this Macchiavellianism, all this rhetoric seems to me to be more an aristocratic pastime for preachers and moralists.

The general foundation of that attitude upon which the moral subjection of man and the 'debasement' of his personality so firmly rest, is almost exclusively the dualism with which all our judgments are imbued. Dualism is Christianity raised to the power of logic, Christianity freed from tradition, from mysticism. Its chief method consists in dividing into spurious antitheses that which is in fact indivisible—for instance body and soul—in pitting these abstractions one against the other, and then effecting an artificial reconciliation between what was always joined in inseparable unity. It is the Gospel myth of God and man reconciled by Christ, translated into philosophical language.

As Christ tramples upon the flesh thereby redeeming the human race, so in dualism idealism sides with one shadow against another, granting spirit the monopoly over matter, species the monopoly over the particular, sacrificing man to the state, the state to humanity.

Imagine now the chaos induced in the minds and consciences of people who from childhood upward have heard nothing else. Dualism has distorted all simple notions to such an extent that people have to make great efforts to master truths as clear as day. Our language is the language of dualism, our imagination has no other images, no other metaphors. For a millenium and a half all teaching, all preaching, all writing, all action, were impregnated with dualism. Only at the end of the eighteenth century did a few men begin to doubt, but, even while doubting, went on, for the sake of respectability, and also partly out of fear, to speak its language.

It goes without saying that our entire morality originates from this same source. This morality demanded constant sacrifice, ceaseless heroism, endless selflessness. That is why its rules were hardly ever obeyed. Life is infinitely more stubborn than theory, it goes its way independent of it and silently conquers it. A fuller protest against accepted morality could not be made than this rejection of it in practice, but people go on living peacefully in this contradiction. They have been used to it for centuries. Christianity, dividing man into, on the one hand, something ideal and, on the other, animal, has confused his understanding. Finding no way out of the struggle between conscience and the passions, he has become so used to hypocrisy, often quite open, that the contradiction between the word and the deed does not disturb him. He pleaded his weak, evil nature, and the church hurried with indulgences and remission of sins to provide an easy way of settling accounts with his frightened conscience, because she feared that otherwise despair might lead him into another way of thinking which might not be so easy to allay with confession and remission. These naughty habits became so rooted that they outlived even the power of the church. Affectation of civic virtue has replaced that of cant; the result—all this theatrical excitement in the style of the Romans, or the Christian martyrs, or feudal knights.

Here, too, practical life goes its own way, taking no interest in heroic morality.

But no one dares attack this morality and it persists, supported on the one side by a secret alliance of pity and respect, like the republic of San Marino, and on the other by our cowardice, our lack of character, our false shame and moral servitude. We are afraid of charges of immorality and that is what curbs us. We repeat the moral gibberish that we hear, attaching no meaning to it, but not protesting against it either, like naturalists who, 'for decency's sake,' introduce God into their prefaces and marvel at His wisdom. The respect inspired in us by terror of the wild clamour of the mob has become so much of a habit that we look with amazement and indignation at the impudence of a sincere and free man who dares to doubt the truth of this rhetoric; such doubt is an affront to us, just as a disrespectful remark about the king was an affront to his subject—it is the pride of a lackey, the arrogance of a slave.

Thus conventional morality was formed, and conventional language; in this language we impart faith in false gods to our children, deceive them as our parents deceived us and as our children will deceive theirs, until a revolution puts an end to this world of lies and deceit.

I can no longer bear this perpetual rhetoric of patriotic and philanthropic phrases that have no influence on life at all. Can you find many people ready to sacrifice their lives for whatever it may be? Not many, of course, but, still, more than those with the courage to say that '*Mourir pour la Patrie*' is not really the apex of human happiness, and that it would be much better if both country and the individual could remain intact.

What children we are, what slaves we still are! And how the whole centre of gravity, the point of support of our will and our morality lie outside us!

This falsehood is not only pernicious, but degrading, it offends our self-respect, it corrupts our behaviour. One must have strength of character to speak and act consistently, and that is why people ought to admit in words what they daily admit to in their lives. Perhaps this sentimental chatter, like superficial politeness, was of some use in more barbarous ages, but now it weakens, lulls, bewilders. Too long have we allowed these rhetorical exercises to be declaimed with impunity, these exercises composed of *réchauffé* Christianity, diluted with the muddy water of rationalism and the sugary flavour of philanthropy. The time has come to examine these sybilline books, to demand a full statement from our teachers.

What is the meaning of all these lucubrations against egoism and individualism?—What is egoism?—What is *brotherhood*?—What is individualism?—And what is love of humanity?

Of course men are egoists, because they are individuals;

how can one be oneself without a sharp consciousness of one's personality? To deprive man of this consciousness is to dissolve him, to turn him into a flat, faded, characterless being. We are egoists—and therefore we fight for independence, for well-being, for the recognition of our rights, that is why we thirst for love, seek action and cannot deny these same rights to others without obvious contradiction.

A century ago, the preaching of individualism awakened people from the heavy slumber into which they had sunk under the influence of the Catholic opiate. It led to freedom just as humility leads to submission. The writings of the egoist Voltaire did more for liberation than those of the loving Rousseau did for brotherhood.

Moralists talk of egoism as of a bad habit, without asking whether man can remain man, having lost a living sense of personality, and without explaining what kind of a substitute 'brotherhood' and 'love of humanity' will prove. They do not even explain why one should be a brother of all and sundry and what is this duty of loving everyone in the world. We equally see no reason to love or hate anything merely because it exists. Leave man free in his emotions. He will find whom to love and whom to be a brother to; for that he does not need commandments or orders and if he doesn't find anyone, that is his affair and his misfortune.

Christianity at least did not stop at such trifles, but boldly ordered men to love not merely everyone but especially enemies. For eighteen hundred years men found this deeply touching; now it is time to admit that this rule is not absolutely clear. . . . Why should we love our enemies? Or if they are so amiable, why be their enemies?

The fact is quite simply that egoism and social sense (brotherhood and love) are not virtues or vices. They are the basic elements of human life, without which there would be no history, no development, but either the scattered life of wild beasts or else a herd of tame troglodytes. Kill the social sense in man—and you will get a savage orang-outang; kill egoism in him, and he will become a tame monkey. Slaves have the least egoism of anyone. The very word 'egoism' hasn't a precise meaning. There is a narrow, bestial, filthy egoism just as there is a filthy, bestial, narrow love. The real point is not to fulminate against egoism and extol brotherhood, for the one will never overcome the other, but to unite freely and harmoniously these two ineradicable elements of human life.

As a social being, man strives to love and needs no commandment to do so. To hate oneself is not at all necessary. Moralists consider all moral action to be so repugnant to human nature that they attribute great merit to every good action. That is why they make brotherhood a duty, like keeping Lent or mortifying the flesh. The last form of the religion of slavery is based on the divorce between society and the individual, on the fictitious hostility between them. As long as there is on one side the Archangel-Brotherhood and on the other Lucifer-Egoism, there will be a government to reconcile them and keep them in leash, there will be judges to punish, executioners to execute, the church to pray God for forgiveness, a God to inspire fear, and the commissar of police to put people in prison.

The harmony between society and the individual is not established once and for all. It *comes into being* in each period, almost in each country, and it changes with circumstances, like everything living. There can be no universal norm, no universal decision in the matter. We have seen how easy it is at some periods for man to surrender to his milieu and how at others he can *preserve* the tie only by exile, by withdrawal—*taking his all with him*. It is not in our power to change the historical relationship of the individual to society, nor unfortunately is it in the power of society itself, but it depends on us whether we are contemporary, in harmony with our development, in a word, whether we *mould* our conduct in response to circumstances.

Indeed, the truly free man *creates* his own morality. That was what the Stoics meant when they said: 'There are no laws for the wise.' What was admirable behaviour yesterday may be abominable to-day. There is no eternal, immutable morality, just as there are no eternal rewards and punishments. That which is really immutable in morality can be reduced to such generalities that almost everything personal in them is lost; for instance, that every action contrary to our convictions is a crime, or, as Kant said, that an act that man cannot universalize or elevate to a rule is immoral.

At the beginning of this article we advised against entering into contradiction with oneself, however high the price, and in favour of breaking all insincere relations supported (as in Benjamin Constant's *Alfred*[1]) by false shame and unnecessary self-sacrifice.

Whether present circumstances are or are not as I have shown them may be disputed, and if you prove me wrong, I shall shake your hand gratefully, you will be my benefactor. Perhaps I have gone too far and while painfully examining the horrors that occur around us, have lost the capacity of seeing the better side. I am ready to listen, I wish to agree. But if circumstances are as I say, then there can be no argument.

'And so,' you will say, 'one should give oneself up to indignant inactivity, become alien to everything, grumble fruitlessly, become cross, as old men do, withdraw from the scene where the stream of life bubbles and boils, and live out one's days useless to others, a burden to oneself?'

My advice is not to quarrel with the world, but to begin an independent, self-reliant life, which would find salvation within itself even were the whole world around us to perish. I advise looking closely into the question whether the masses are really moving where we think they are moving, whether we should go with them or away from them, but knowing where they are going; I advise abandoning bookish

[1] i.e. *Adolphe*.

opinions that have been inculcated into us from childhood, opinions that represent men as completely different from what they really are. I want to put an end to 'fruitless grumbling and peevish discontent'; I want to reconcile people with themselves, having convinced them that they cannot be better and that it is not their fault that they are as they are.

Whether this will involve this or that kind of external action or none at all I do not know and, anyhow, this is not important. If you are stronger, if there is something in you, not only of value, but something that will stir others profoundly, it will not be lost, such is the economy of nature. Your strength, like a pinch of yeast, will surely agitate, ferment all that comes under its influence; your actions, thoughts, words will take their place without any special effort. If you have no such strength or strength of a kind that has no effect on contemporary man, that is not a great misfortune either for you or for others. What are we but everlasting comedians, but men of the streets! We do not live to entertain others, we live for ourselves. The majority of people, always practical, do not bother at all about the lack of *historical* activity.

Instead of assuring the people that they passionately want what we want, it would be better for us to ask ourselves whether they want something different, or whether they want anything at all at this moment, then to concentrate, to pack up shop, to leave in peace, without doing violence to others or wasting ourselves.

Maybe this negative action will be the beginning of a new life. In any case, it will be a virtuous act.

PARIS, Hôtel Mirabeau, 1850
April 3rd

VII

EPILOGUE 1849

Opfer fallen hier,
Weder Lamm noch Stier,
Aber Menschenopfer—unerhört.
GOETHE—Die Braut von Corinth

A CURSE upon you, year of blood and madness, year of triumphant vulgarity, bestiality, stupidity—a curse upon you!

From the first day to the last you brought only misery; not one bright minute, not one peaceful hour did you contain. From the revival of the guillotine in Paris, from the Bourges trial [1] to the gallows which the English provided for the children of Cephalonia,[2] from the bullets with which the King of Prussia's brother executed the citizens of Baden, from Rome falling to the betrayers of humanity, to Hungary sold to the enemy by a general who had betrayed his country, everything about you was criminal, bloody, revolting, everything was stamped with the seal of apostasy. And this is only the first step, the beginning, the prelude. The years to come will be more disgusting, more brutal, more degrading. . . .

To what an age of tears and despair have we come. . . . The mind reels, the heart aches, it is frightening to know what is going on, and frightening not to know what fresh

[1]March 7th–April 2nd, 1849: Blanqui, Barbès and Raspail were sent to prison for the Paris Demonstration of May 15th, 1848 in favour of the re-establishment of Poland.

[2]One of the Ionian islands under the English domination, where in 1848 revolts for national independence were suppressed.

horrors have been perpetrated. The seething venom within one drives one to hatred and contempt; humiliation gnaws at one's vitals, and one wants to escape . . . to be off . . . to give up—to vanish without trace, without knowing it.

The last hope to warm and sustain one—the hope of revenge, a wild, insane, unnecessary revenge, but one which would prove that modern man has a heart—is receding. The soul is sere, there is not a green leaf left. All is scattered . . . all is silence . . . the mist and the cold are rising. . . . All one hears is from time to time the thud of the executioner's axe as it falls, or the whistle of a bullet—the executioner's bullet—in search of the noble breast of some youth, killed because he believed in humanity.

And will they not be avenged? . . .

Had they no friend, no brother? Are there no men who share their faith?—All this there is, only revenge there will not be!

From their ashes there rose, not Marius, but an entire literature of after-dinner speeches, lucubrations of demagogues—including my own—and prosy verse.

They do not know this. How fortunate that they are no more, and that there is no life beyond the grave. For *they* believed in men, believed that there was something to die for, and their death was noble, holy, redeeming a feeble generation of eunuchs. We hardly know their names. The murder of Robert Blum [1] amazed and shocked us, then we grew used to it. . . .

I feel ashamed of our generation: we seem mere soulless orators. Our blood is cold, only our ink is hot; our minds are in a constant state of ineffectual irritation, our mouths are filled with passionate words with no influence on action.

[1]Robert Blum (1807–48), German radical journalist and agitator. Vice-president of Provisional Parliament at Frankfurt, 1848. Carried German memorial of congratulation to Vienna insurgents, October 1848. Shot the next month by Windishgrätz when the city was recaptured.

When we should strike we reflect, we calculate when we should be impulsive; we are hideously rational and are haughty about everything, we endure everything, we are interested only in the *Universal*, the *Idea*, *Humanity*.

> Our loves and hatreds are chance encounters.
> We pledge nothing to malice or to love.

We have wasted our spirit in the regions of the abstract and general just as the monks let it wither in the world of prayer and contemplation. We have lost our taste for reality, come out above it, just as the bourgeoisie came out below it.

And what were you doing, revolutionaries, scared of the revolution? Political *gamins*, clowns of freedom, you played at Republic, at Terror, at Government. You made fools of yourselves in the clubs, chattered in the Chambers, rattled on in your parliaments, dressed up as buffoons with pistols and sabres, took chaste pleasure in the fact that open scoundrels, astonished to be alive, extolled your mercy. You anticipated nothing, you foresaw nothing. And some, *the best among you*, paid with their heads for your lunacy. Take a lesson now from your enemies, who defeated you because they are cleverer than you. See if *they* are afraid of reaction, afraid of going too far, of soiling their hands with blood. They are up to their elbows, up to their necks, in blood. Wait a little—they will execute you all, you are not out of their reach. Execute indeed—they will simply whip you like curs.

I am truly horrified by modern man. Such absence of feeling, such narrowness of outlook, such lack of passion and indignation, such feebleness of thought. How quickly all impulse cools, how quickly wane his energy, his enthusiasm, his faith in his own activity. But when, how did these people waste their lives? When did they have time to dissipate their strength? They were corrupted at school and befuddled there. They went to pieces, with their existence of beer-shops and wild student squalor. They lost their strength in petty, dirty amours. Born and bred in a sick-room atmosphere, they never had much energy and withered before they blossomed. They were exhausted, not by passion but by dreams of passion. Here again, as always, these *litterateurs*, men of letters, idealists, theorists practised debauchery in their minds and passion in books. Really one sometimes bitterly regrets that a man cannot transfer to some other species of animal. . . . Obviously to be a donkey, a frog, or a dog is pleasanter, honester, nobler than to be a man of the nineteenth century.

No one is to blame. It is neither their fault, nor ours. It is the misfortune of being born when a whole world is dying.

Only one consolation remains: it is highly probable that the generations to come will degenerate even more, will grow shallower, poorer in mind and heart. Even our achievements will be beyond them, and our ideas impossible for them to understand. Peoples, like royal houses, grow stupid before the collapse. Their minds grow dark, they fall into dotage, like those Merovingians who were conceived in debauchery and incest, and expired in a kind of coma without ever having come to their senses; like an aristocracy that has degenerated into weak-minded cretins, stunted in growth, their features deformed, bourgeois Europe will live out her miserable days in the twilight of imbecility, in sluggish feelings without conviction, without fine arts, without powerful poetry. Weak, sickly, foolish generations will somehow stretch on until the eruption, until some lava or other will encase them in stone and commit them to the oblivion of chronicles.

And then. . . ?

And then spring will come, life will play on their tombstones; the barbarism of infancy, full of chaotic but healthy forces, will replace senile barbarism. Wild, fresh strength will well out of the young breast of youthful nations and a new cycle of events will begin and with it the third volume of universal history.

We can already see what its general tone will be. It will be connected with social ideas. This socialism will develop in all its phases until it reaches its own extremes and absurdities. Then once again a cry of denial will break from the titanic chest of the revolutionary minority and again a mortal struggle will begin, in which socialism will play the rôle of contemporary conservatism and will be overwhelmed in the subsequent revolution, as yet unknown to us. The eternal play of life, ruthless as death, inevitable as birth, the *corsi e ricorsi* of history, the *perpetuum mobile* of the pendulum.

Towards the end of the eighteenth century the European Sisyphus rolled his stone, composed of the ruins and fragments of three heterogeneous worlds, up to the summit. The stone rocked, first to one side, then to the other, looked as if it might come to rest. But far from it. It rolled over, and, imperceptibly, began to go down; perhaps it might have caught on something, and come to a stop with such brakes and obstacles as representative government, constitutional monarchy. Then it would have weathered there for centuries accepting every change as a step towards perfection, every movement as progress—like that China in Europe known as England, like that antediluvian State situated amid antediluvian mountains, called Switzerland. But for this it was necessary that no wind blow, that there be no jolt, no shock; but the wind blew, the jolt came. The February storm shook the whole inherited fabric. The storm of the June days finally loosened the whole mass of Romano-feudal deposit and it slid downhill with gathering speed, smashing everything in its way and smashing itself to pieces. . . . Poor Sisyphus looks on and cannot believe his eyes. His face is haggard, the sweat of exhaustion mingles with the sweat of horror, tears of despair, shame, impotence and frustration stand in his eyes. He had such faith in perfectibility, in humanity; he had believed in modern man so philosophically, so intelligently, so eruditely! And still he was mistaken.

The French revolution and German science are the pillars of Hercules of the European world. Beyond them, on the other side, opens the ocean, the new world can be discerned—something different, not a mere emended edition of old Europe. It promised the world emancipation from church oppression, from political slavery, from moral authority. But while sincerely proclaiming freedom of thought and freedom of life, the men of the revolution did not realize quite how incompatible all this was with the Catholic order in Europe. Repudiate this order as yet they could not. In order to go forward, they had to roll up their banner, betray it, compromise.

Rousseau and Hegel—are Christians.

Robespierre and St Just—are Monarchists.

German science is a speculative religion, the republic of the Convention is the absolutism of the Pentarchy and at the same time a Church. In place of the Creed there appeared civil dogmas. The Assembly and the Government officiated at the mystery of the people's liberation. The legislator became the priest, the seer, and enunciated benevolently and without irony eternal, infallible judgments in the name of popular sovereignty.

The people, of course, remained, as before, the *laity*, the *governed*. For them nothing was changed and they attended the political liturgies understanding nothing, just as they had the religious ones. But the terrible word, Liberty, became involved in the world of habit, ritual and authority. It entered into people's hearts, it resounded in their ears, it could not remain inactive; it fermented, it eroded the foundations of the social edifice; it was enough to inject it in one spot or decompose one drop of the old blood. With this poison in its veins, the old body could not be saved. After the demented period of the Empire the consciousness of impending danger was forcibly evident. All the profound intellects of the day waited for the cataclysm and were afraid of it. The legitimist Chateaubriand and Lammenais, then still an abbé, pointed to it. The bloodthirsty terrorist of Catholicism, Maistre, in his fear of it, stretched out one hand to the Pope, the other to the hangman. Hegel furled the sails of his philosophy, sailing so proudly and freely on the seas of logic, afraid of going too far from shore and being caught in a squall. Niebuhr, troubled by the same foreboding, died after seeing 1830 and the July revolution. A whole school was established in Germany[1] which aspired to arrest the future by means of the past, to bar the door to the new-born with the father's corpse—*Vanitas Vanitatum!*

Two giants finally arrived to round off triumphantly this phase of history.

The venerable figure of Goethe, unconcerned with the turmoil around him, aloof from his environment, stands calmly at the entrance to our age, closing the door to two past ages. He overshadows his contemporaries and reconciles them with the past. The old man was still alive when there appeared and vanished the only poet of the nineteenth century, the poet of doubt and indignation, confessor, executioner and victim in one. He hurriedly read a sceptical prayer for the dying over the senile world and died at the age of thirty-seven in a renascent Greece, where he had fled only in order not to see 'his country's shores'.

After him, everything died down. No one seemed to notice the sterility of the century, the complete absence of creativeness. At first it was still illuminated by the afterglow of the eighteenth century, it basked in its glory, it took pride in its sons. As these stars from another heaven faded, twilight and gloom descended upon everything. Everywhere impotence, meanness and mediocrity and, in the

[1]The reference is to the German historical school of Jurisprudence.

east, a barely perceptible thread of light, with its hint of distant dawn, before the breaking of which many a thunder cloud would burst.

At last prophets appeared who foretold imminent disaster and distant redemption. They were thought crazed, their new idiom aroused anger, their words were taken for ravings. A crowd does not wish to be awakened, all it asks is to be left in peace with its wretched way of life, with its vulgar habits. Like Frederick II it wants to die without changing its dirty underclothes. Nothing in the world could satisfy this modest desire so well as the bourgeois monarchy.

But disintegration duly went on, the 'underground mole' was working indefatigably. All institutions, all authorities were eaten out by the secret cancer. On February 24th, 1848, the illness changed from a chronic to an acute condition. The French Republic was proclaimed to the world with the trumpet of the day of doom. The impotence, the decrepitude of the old social order became obvious, everything began to fall to pieces and dissolve, everything has become confused and is kept going by this very confusion. Revolutionaries have become conservatives, conservatives—anarchists. The republic has destroyed the last of the free institutions that survived under the monarchy, the country of Voltaire has abandoned itself to cant. Everything and everyone has been conquered, but there is no conqueror! . . .

To the many who still hoped, we said—this is not recovery, but the flush of consumption. Bold in our thoughts, impudent in our speech, we were not afraid to analyse the evil, or to describe it, but now a cold sweat stands out on our foreheads. I am the first to blanch and tremble, before the dark night that is descending. I shudder at the thought that our prophecies are being fulfilled so rapidly, that their accomplishment is so inevitable.

Farewell, departing world, farewell, Europe!

But what shall we do with ourselves?

. . . We shall be the last links joining two worlds, belonging neither to the one nor to the other; men severed from our kind, divided from our environment and abandoned to ourselves; superfluous because we can share neither the senility of the one side, nor the infancy of the other. There is no room for us at any table. Men who deny the past, men who have only abstract plans for the future, we have no heritage in either, and therein lies testimony both to our strength and to its uselessness.

If only we could go away! With our lives, begin the liberation, the protest, the new ways of life. As if we were really so free of the old world! Do not our virtues and our vices, our passions, above all our habits still belong to that world with which we have broken only in our convictions?

What shall we do in virgin forests, we who cannot spend a morning without reading five newspapers, we whose whole poetry is in the struggle with the old world. . . . No, let us be frank and admit that we would make poor Robinson Crusoes.

And those who went to America, did they not take old England with them there?

But would we not go on hearing distant groans? Could we turn away, shut our eyes, stop up our ears, decide to know nothing, preserve a stubborn silence—i.e., admit defeat and surrender? Impossible! Our enemies must know that there exist independent human beings who will never give up free speech, not for anything, not until an axe has passed between their head and their body, not before a rope has wrung their necks.

Therefore let our words be heard!

. . . But whom shall we talk to? . . . About what? . . . I really have no notion, only this is something stronger than I. . . .

ZURICH, 1849
December 21st

VIII

DONOSO-CORTES, MARQUÈS DE VALDEGAMAS,[1] AND JULIAN, ROMAN EMPEROR

THE conservatives have eyes, but they see not. Greater sceptics than the Apostle Thomas, they put their finger in the wound but do not believe in it.

'Look,' they say, 'at the dreadful progress of the social gangrene; at the spirit of denial which exhales corruption; at the demon of revolution, shaking the ultimate foundations of the ancient edifice of the state. . . . You see now—our world is disintegrating, perishing, dragging down with it education, institutions, everything that it has established. See, it has already one foot in the grave.'

And, thereupon conclude, 'So let us double the strength of the state by means of the army, let us bring back people to the faith that they lack. The salvation of the entire world is at stake.'

To save the world by memories, by violence! The world is saved by 'good tidings', not by *réchauffé* religion. It is saved by the *word* bearing within it the seed of the new world, not by resurrecting the old world.

What is it—stubbornness on their part, a lack of understanding or terror before the gloomy future that troubles them to such a point that they see only what is perishing, are tied only to what is past, and lean only on ruins or on walls ready to crumble. What chaos, what inconsequence in the ideas of modern man!

[1]Juan-Francisco-Maria de la Salud-Donoso-Cortes, Marquès de Valdegamas, Spanish statesman.

At least there was some sort of unity in the past, the lunacy was epidemic and not much noticed. The whole world was in error, there were common assumptions, for the most part absurd, but accepted by all. In our day, it is not so; the prejudices of the Roman world alongside the prejudices of the Middle Ages, the Gospel and political economy, Loyola and Voltaire, idealism in theory and materialism in practice, an abstract rhetorical morality and behaviour directly opposed to it. All these heterogenous ideas live together in our minds without order. Now that we have come of age, we are too busy, too lazy and perhaps too cowardly to submit our moral rules to any rigorous scrutiny, and so everything remains in twilight.

Nowhere does this mishmash of ideas go so far as in France. The French in general have no philosophical education; with great sagacity they master conclusions but only in a one-sided way; their conclusions remain disconnected, without any unity to link them together, without even being reduced to the same level; hence contradictions at every step, and the necessity when talking with them to go back to old familiar principles and to repeat, as if they were novel, truths enunciated by Spinoza and Bacon.

As they embrace conclusions divorced from their grounds, there is nothing that they positively acquire in them, nothing completed, neither in science nor in life ... completed in the sense in which the four rules of arithmetic are, or some quasi-scientific principles in Germany, or some of the principles of law in England. This is in part a cause of that liability to change, that tendency to go from one extreme to another, which so surprises us. A generation of revolutionaries become absolutists; after a series of revolutions the same questions are asked again: Should the rights of man be recognized? Can one pronounce judgments outside the forms of law? Should one tolerate freedom of the press? The fact that these questions reappear after each upheaval, makes it clear that not one of them has been properly considered, let alone answered.

This intellectual confusion Cousin[1] presented as an organized system under the name of Eclecticism (i.e. a little goes a long way). In life, it is equally at home amongst radicals and legitimists, and particularly amongst *moderates*, i.e. amongst people who know neither what they want nor what they do not want.

All the royalist and Catholic journals join in one great chorus of praise for Donoso-Cortes' speech, delivered in Madrid at the meeting of the Cortes. And this speech really is remarkable in many respects. Donoso-Cortes has diagnosed with unusual accuracy the present terrible condition of the European states; he has seen that they are on the edge of an abyss, on the eve of an unavoidable, fatal cataclysm. The picture he draws is terrifying in its truth. He depicts a Europe which has lost its way, impotent, drawn rapidly towards disaster, dying of lack of order, and over against it, the Slav world ready to overwhelm the Germano-Roman world. He says: 'Do not think that this will be the end of the catastrophe. The Slav tribes are not to the West what the Germans were to the Romans. The Slavs have long been in contact with revolution. Russia, in the midst of a Europe subjugated and rolling in the dust, will absorb through all its pores the poison of which Europe has already drunk deep, and it will kill her. She will decompose in the same way. I do not know what remedies God has prepared against this universal disintegration.'

While we await this divine panacea, do you know what our gloomy prophet proposes—the prophet who has depicted the lineaments of approaching death with such terrible accuracy? We blush to repeat it. He thinks that if England returned to Catholicism, the whole of Europe

[1]Victor Cousin (1792–1867). Professor of philosophy in Paris and prolific author of works chiefly notable for their wide influence and total lack of originality.

could be saved by the Pope, the power of the monarchy and the army. He wants to avert the terrifying future by withdrawing into the impossible past.

There is something suspect about the pathology of the Marquès de Valdegamas. Either the danger is not so great or the remedy is ineffectual. The principle of monarchy has been everywhere restored, the army is everywhere dominant, the church, in Donoso-Cortes' own words and in those of his friend Montalembert, is triumphant. Thiers has become a Catholic. In short, it would be hard to wish for more oppression, more persecution, more reaction, and yet still salvation does not come. Can it really be because England persists in her sinful apostasy?

Every day socialists are blamed for being good only at criticism, at the denunciation of evil, at denial. What would you say now about our anti-social enemies?

To complete this absurdity, the editors of one very white journal [1] published in the same issue some fulsome praise of Donoso-Cortes' speech and also some excerpts from a short historical compilation of a rather mediocre kind, dealing with the early centuries of Christianity and Julian the Apostate, which triumphantly destroys the theory of the Marquès.

Donoso-Cortes takes up exactly the same position as the Roman conservatives of that period. He has seen, as they saw, the social order of the day disintegrating. And he is terrified, which is quite natural; for there is something to be afraid of. He wants, as they did, to save it at whatever cost, and finds no other way but to stop the future, to divert it, as though it were not the natural consequence of the present.

He starts, as the Romans did, from a common assumption, which is quite erroneous, from an unverified hypothesis, from arbitrary opinion. He is convinced that the present forms of social life, as they have developed under the influence of Roman, German, Christian principles, are the only possible ones. As if the ancient world and the con-

[1] *Le Constitutionel.*

temporary Orient did not present us with examples of social life based on quite different principles, perhaps lower, inferior, but extremely secure!

Donoso-Cortes further supposes that education cannot develop otherwise than in the contemporary European forms. It is easy to say with Donoso-Cortes that the ancient world had culture, but not civilization (*le monde ancien était cultivé, non civilisé*). Such subtleties are impressive only in theological disputation. Rome and Greece were highly educated, their education was, like that of Europe, the culture of a minority. Here the arithmetical difference is not important. And yet their life lacked the most essential element of all—Catholicism!

Donoso-Cortes, always standing with his back to the future, sees only disintegration and decay; then the invasion of the Russians; and then barbarism. Astounded by this terrible fate, he seeks means of salvation, *points d'appui*, something firm and healthy in this agonized world, and finds nothing. He turns for help to moral and physical death, to the priest and the soldier.

What kind of social order is it that has to be saved by such means as these, and be it what it may be, is it worth ransoming at this price?

We agree with Donoso-Cortes that Europe, as she is to-day, is crumbling away. From their first appearance socialists have constantly said this; on this they all agree. The chief difference between them and political revolutionaries is that the latter wish to correct and improve the existing order, preserving the old foundations, whereas socialism completely renounces the old order with its law and representative government, with its church and its tribunal, with its civil and criminal codes, renounces it totally, as the early Christians renounced the Roman world.

Such a renunciation is not the caprice of a diseased imagination, not the cry of an individual insulted by society, but the death sentence of this society, the premonition of the end, the realization of the disease dragging the decrepit world to its doom and to resurrection in other forms. The contemporary state will fall before the protest of socialism, its strength is spent, what it could give it has given. Now it is living on its own flesh and blood, it is incapable of developing any further or of arresting development. It has no more to say or do and so it has concentrated all its energy on conservatism, on defence of its position. To stop the fulfilment of a particular destiny is to some degree feasible. History has not that strict, unalterable determination, which is taught by Catholics and preached by philosophers. Into the formula of its development there enter many variable factors—first and foremost the will and power of the individual.

It is possible to lead astray an entire generation, to strike it blind, to drive it insane, to direct it towards a false goal. Napoleon proved this.

Reaction does not command even these means. Donoso-Cortes found only the Catholic church and monarchist barracks. And since to believe or not to believe does not depend on the tyrant's whim, there remain violence, terror, persecution, and extermination.

Much is forgiven to development, to progress, but nevertheless when terror is introduced in the name of success and freedom, it justly provokes general execration. And this is the method that reaction wants to use in order to maintain that existing order whose decrepitude and decay our orator proclaims with such energy. Terror is invoked not in order to go forward, but in order to go back. They want to kill the child in order to feed a dying old man, to revive his failing strength for a moment.

How much blood must be shed to return to the happy days of the Edict of Nantes or the Spanish Inquisition! I do not for a moment think it impossible to arrest the course of humanity, but this is impossible without repeating the Eve of St Bartholomew. It would be necessary to annihilate, to beat to death, to exile, to throw into jail everything that is thinking and active in our generation. The people must be pushed into even deeper ignorance and all that is strongest in them press-ganged into the army. One would have to commit moral infanticide over a whole generation. And all this in order to save an exhausted social structure which satisfies neither *you* nor *us*. Where, then, lies the difference between Russian barbarism and Catholic civilization?

To sacrifice thousands of men, the development of a whole epoch, to a Moloch of statehood as though that were the whole purpose of our life. . . . Have you thought about it, you Christians who love mankind? To sacrifice others and be self-sacrificing on their behalf is too easy to be a virtue. It sometimes happens that amid popular storms long-suppressed passions are unleashed, bloody and merciless, vengeful and indomitable. We understand them with heads bowed in horror, but we do not elevate them to a general law and do not indicate them as a method.

But is this not the real meaning of the encomium that Donoso-Cortes addresses to the obedient and unquestioning soldier on whose rifle he rests half his hopes. He says that 'the priest and the soldier are a great deal closer to one another than is usually believed'. He compares this innocent murderer, sentenced to his crime by society, to a monk, a living corpse. Terrible admission! The two extremes of a dying world join hands, meeting like the two enemies in Byron's *Darkness*. Upon the ruins of a dying world, to encompass its salvation, the last representative of intellectual slavery unites himself with the last representative of physical coercion.

The church became reconciled to the soldier as soon as it became a state church, but it never dared admit to this betrayal. It understood how much in this alliance was false and hypocritical; this was one of the thousands of concessions that it made to the despised earthly world. We shall not reproach it for that, for it was compelled to accept much that went against its teaching. Christian morality has always been only a noble dream never realized.

But the Marquès de Valdegamas bravely set the soldier by the side of the priest, the guardroom next to the altar, the gospel which remits sins beside the army manual which shoots dead for offences. The time has come for us to sing a 'Requiem' or, rather, a 'Te Deum'. This is the end of the church and the end of the army.

At last the masks are off. The players have recognized one another. Of course, the priest and the soldier are brothers, both are unfortunate children of moral darkness, of that insane dualism in which mankind is struggling and losing all its strength. He who says: 'Love thy neighbour and obey authority' is, in effect, saying: 'Obey authority and shoot thy neighbour.'

Christian crucifying of the flesh is as much against nature as the crucifying of others to order. It was necessary to corrupt and confound all our simplest notions, everything that is called conscience, in order to persuade people that murder without ill-will, without knowing why, against one's conviction, could be a sacred duty. All this rests on the same foundation, on the same fundamental error that has cost humanity so much tears and so much blood. All this comes from contempt for the earth and the temporal, from adoration of heaven and the eternal, from lack of respect for individuals and from reverence for the state. All those maxims like *Salus populi suprema lex*, *Pereat mundus et fiat justitia*, have about them a strong smell of burnt flesh, of blood, inquisition, torture, and in general the *triumph of order*.

But why did Donoso-Cortes forget the third brother, the third guardian angel of crumbling government—the hangman? Was it because the hangman is becoming more and more identified with the soldier thanks to the rôle he is forced to play?

All the virtues, admired by Donoso-Cortes, are modestly

united in the hangman, and moreover to the highest degree: obedience to authority, blind execution of orders, unlimited self-dedication. He does not need the faith of the priest, nor the enthusiasm of the soldier. He kills in cold blood, with calculation, without danger to himself, like the law, in the name of society and order. He enters into an unequal competition with every criminal, and always wins, because he has the whole state behind him. He has not the pride of the priest, nor the ambition of the soldier. He does not expect a reward either from God or man; there is no glory or honour for him on earth, no promise of paradise in heaven, he sacrifices everything: his name, his honour, his dignity. He hides from the sight of man, and all this so as to mete out solemn justice to the enemies of society.

Let us render the man of social vengeance his due and say, imitating our orator: 'The hangman is a great deal closer to the priest than is usually believed.'

The hangman has a great part to play every time it becomes necessary to crucify 'a new man', or behead some old crowned phantom. Maistre did not forget him in speaking of the Pope.

And apropos of Golgotha, I have remembered a fragment about the persecution of the early Christians. Read it, or, even better, take the writings of the early Fathers, Tertullian or one of the Roman conservatives. How like the present struggle—the same passions, the same power on one side, and the same resistance on the other. Even the expressions used are the same. If one reads the accusations brought against the Christians by Celsus or Julian, of immorality, mad utopias, murder of children and corruption of adults, destruction of the state, religion, the family, why, it seems to be a Premier-Paris of the *Constitutionel* or the *Assemblée Nationale*, only more intelligently written.

If the friends of order in Rome did not preach the massacre and extermination of the Nazarenes, this was only because the pagan world was more human, not so spiritual, less intolerant than the Catholic bourgeoisie. Ancient Rome did not know the strong methods invented by the Western Church and so successfully adopted in the extermination of the Albigenses and on the Eve of St Bartholomew, to the glory of which there are still frescoes [1] in the Vatican, showing the god-fearing purification of the streets of Paris from the Huguenots, those same streets which the bourgeoisie a year ago so zealously cleared of socialists. However, the spirit is the same, and the difference much a matter of circumstances and personality. As a matter of fact the difference is all in our favour: comparing the reports of Bauchart [2] with those of Pliny the Younger, the magnanimity of the Emperor Trajan who loathed denunciations against Christians with the inexorability of the Emperor Cavaignac who did not share this particular prejudice in the case of socialists, we see that the dying order has fallen so low that it cannot find any advocates like Trajan, nor any secretaries of committees of inquiry like Pliny.

The police measures are also similar. Christian clubs were suppressed by soldiers as soon as they came to the notice of the authorities. Christians were condemned unheard, they were accused on trifling charges for outward signs, they were refused the right to expound their teaching. Tertullian was outraged by this, as we all are now, and this inspired his *apologias* to the Roman Senate. Christians were thrown to the wild beasts who, for this purpose, played the part of police-troops in Rome. Propaganda grows stronger, degrading punishments no longer degrade—on the contrary, the condemned become heroes, like the convicts of Bourges.

[1] Herzen refers to the frescoes in the Sala Regia depicting the Massacre of St Bartholomew by Vasari.

[2] Alexandre Quentin-Bouchart (1809–97). French lawyer, prominent in campaign of the banquets. A strong supporter of Cavaignac, he drew up official report on May and June risings of 1848 for which he was savagely attacked by Victor Hugo and Louis Blanc. Although originally hostile to Louis-Napoleon's *coup d'état,* he later enjoyed an eminent official career under the Empire.

Seeing the futility of all these measures, the greatest defender of order, religion and state, Diocletian, decided to deal a crushing blow at the seditious teaching. With sword and fire he attacked the Christians.

And how did it all end? What did the conservatives do with their civilization (or culture?), with their legions, their legislation, their lictors, hangmen, wild beasts, murders and other horrors? They merely provided evidence of how far the ferocity and brutality of conservatism can go, of what a terrible instrument a soldier is, blindly obeying the judge who makes him a hangman, and thereby proved even more clearly the total ineffectiveness of all these measures against the *word*, when its hour has struck.

We may note that at times the ancient world was right as against Christianity, which undermined it in the name of a utopian and impossible doctrine. Sometimes our own conservatives may also be right in their attacks on specific social doctrines . . . but what use was it to them to be right? The days of Rome were drawing to a close, the day of the gospel was dawning.

And all these horrors, bloodshed, butcheries and persecution culminated in the famous cry of despair of the most intelligent of revolutionaries, Julian the Apostate, in the cry: 'Thou hast conquered, Galilean!'[1]

[1]The speech of Donoso-Cortes, Spanish envoy first in Berlin then in Paris, was published in a very large edition at the expense of the Society of the rue Poitiers, notorious for its nullity and its squandering of money on nonsense. I was in Paris at the time and in very close contact with Proudhon's journal. The editors suggested that I should write a reply. Proudhon liked it, but the *Patrie* was furious and in the evening, after repeating what I had said about 'the third defender of society', asked the Prosecutor of the Republic whether he would prosecute an article in which a soldier is compared to a hangman (*bourreau*) and the hangman is called a *hangman* (*bourreau*) and not *the performer of supreme achievements* (*éxecuteur des hautes œuvres*). The denunciation of the police journal had its effect. Next day there was not one copy left in the editorial office out of forty thousand, the usual circulation of the *Voix de Peuple*.—A.H.

THE RUSSIAN PEOPLE AND SOCIALISM

An Open Letter to Jules Michelet

SIR,

You occupy so high a place in the general esteem, everything that you write is received by European Democracy with that unbounded confidence which your noble pen has won for you as a right, that I cannot refrain from replying to you on a matter which touches upon my most deep-seated convictions: on, that is, the description of the Russian people that appears in your noble work on Kosciusko.[1]

A reply is all the more necessary, since it is time that Europe was made to realize that nowadays speaking about Russia is no longer a matter of speaking about a country that is absent, distant, mute.

For we are present, we who have left our country only so that free Russian speech may be heard in Europe. And we hold it our duty to speak out when a man, who quite rightly enjoys such immense authority, tells us that 'he knows—that he swears to it—that he can prove that Russia doesn't exist, that the Russians are not human, that they are devoid of all moral sense.'

Do you mean by this official Russia, the Empire of façades, the Byzantine-German government? If so, you are right. We agree in advance with everything you say. We feel no need to rush into the breach. The Russian government has enough agents in the Paris press to provide a permanent stream of eloquent justifications of its doings.

But it is not only official society that you deal with in your book. You have taken the problem and have gone to its very roots. You have written about the People.

The poor Russian people has no one of its own to raise a voice in its defence. I ask you, then—can we, in such circumstances, without gross cowardice, stay silent?

[1] *Poland & Russia: a Legend of Kosciusko.*

The Russian people, Sir, does exist. It lives. It is not even very old. It is very young. Sometimes (it is true) one dies young, before one has had time to live. It can happen, but not in the ordinary run of events.

For the Russian people the past is dark: the present is terrible: but for all that, it lays some claim to the future, it *has no belief* in its present condition. It has the audacity to hope: and it hopes all the more, since it possesses so little.

The most difficult period for the Russian people is drawing to a close. A terrible struggle lies ahead of it. And this is the moment for which its enemies have been preparing for a hundred years.

The great question, Russia's 'to be or not to be', will soon be resolved. But before the battle, one has no right to despair of the outcome.

The Russian question is assuming grave and disturbing proportions. People of all parties feel concern about it. But it seems that in doing so, they concern themselves too much with the official Russia, the Russia of the Tsar, and too little with the unknown Russia, the Russia of the people.

But even if you insist on looking at Russia solely from the point of view of its government, do you not think that it would be as well to have a rather better knowledge of this uncomfortable neighbour who has mastered the art of infiltrating into every corner of Europe, here with spies, there with bayonets? The Russian government reaches out to the Mediterranean as protector of the Ottoman Porte, to the Rhine as protector of its German uncles and connexions, to the Atlantic as the protector of ORDER in France.

It would be as well, I say, to form a true estimate of this universal protector, and to discover whether this mysterious empire has in fact any other justification for its existence than that of fulfilling the repulsive vocation that the St Petersburg Government has assumed: that of being a barrier cast across the high road of human progress.

Europe is approaching a terrible cataclysm. The world of the Middle Ages has come to an end. The world of feudalism is expiring. The religious and political revolutions are petering out under the weight of their own complete impotence. They have great achievements to their credit, but they have failed to complete their tasks. They have stripped Throne and Altar of the prestige they once enjoyed, but they have not established the era of freedom. They have lit new desires in the hearts of men but they have not provided ways of satisfying them. Parliamentarianism, Protestantism—these are mere prevarications, temporary measures, attempts to stave off the flood, which can arrest only for a short while the process of death and rebirth. The time for them has passed. Since 1848 it has become apparent that no amount of delving into Roman law, of barren casuistry, of thin philosophic deism, of sterile religious rationalism can hold back society from fulfilling its destiny.

The storm draws near. There can no longer be doubt about it; on this point revolutionaries and reactionaries agree. Men's minds are unbalanced: a serious question, a question of life and death, lies heavy on their hearts. Men grow worried, disturbed. They ask themselves, is it still possible for Europe, that hoary Proteus, that decaying organism, to find within itself the strength to bring about its own recovery? And having asked the question, they dread the answer. They tremble with suspense.

It *is* a grave question.

Will old Europe find the means to rid itself of its sluggish blood, so that it may plunge headlong into the limitless future—the future, that passionate, fatal creature who draws us all towards her with irresistible force, towards whom we fling ourselves with utter recklessness, not caring whether our path is driven across the ruins of our ancestral homes, whether we have to squander the treasure of ancient civilizations and the material wealth of modern culture?

On both sides the position is fully understood. Europe

has slipped back into the grim, unbroken darkness that must come before the dawn of the final struggle It is not life but mere suspense, anxiety. Everything is upside down. There is no regard for law, no justice, not even a semblance of liberty. A secular and irreligious inquisition reigns supreme: civil rights have been suspended, and in their stead martial law and a state of siege proclaimed. There is only one moral force that still has any authority over men, that still demands and receives their obedience: and that is Fear, which is universal. All other issues have to give way before the over-riding interest of Reaction. Governments that to all appearances are sharply divided on questions of principle, come together affectionately to form a single œcumenical police force. The Emperor of Russia, without troubling to conceal his loathing for the French, rewards the Prefect of the Paris police: the King of Naples confers a decoration on the President of the Republic with his own hand—the hand of a turnkey: the King of Prussia muffles himself up in his Russian uniform and hurries off to Warsaw to embrace his old enemy the Emperor of Austria and receive the blessing of Nicholas—Nicholas, the heretical Emperor, who, to complete the picture, lends out his soldiers to protect the Roman Pontiff. On this witches' Sabbath, on this Walpurgis night of reaction, all personal security vanishes: safeguards that exist even in the most backward societies, in China, in Persia, are no longer respected in the capitals of what was once the civilized world.

We can no longer believe our eyes. Is this really the Europe that we once knew and loved?

Indeed if there were no longer an England, free and proud, if that diamond set in the silver sea,[1] as Shakespeare called it, no longer shone bright: if Switzerland were to deny its principles time and time again, like St Peter in fear of Caesar: if Piedmont, the one free, strong element in Italy,

[1]"Diamant enchâssé dans l'argent de la mer."

the last refuge of civilization which, expelled from the North, shelters south of the Alps but without daring to cross the Appenines, were suddenly to grow insensible to all human feelings—if in a word, these three countries were to fall victims to that pestilential air which blows from Paris and Vienna, then we should have to say that the dissolution of the old world was complete, that the parricidal hands of the conservatives had done their worst and that barbarism was already upon us in France and Germany.

Turning away from this chaos, from the writhings of insanity and the tears and pains of childbirth, turning away from this world as it falls into rotting pieces by the cradle's side, men's eyes turn involuntarily to the East.

There, like some dark mountain emerging from the mists, may be discerned the unfriendly, menacing contours of an empire: it seems to advance upon one like an avalanche—or like an impatient heir anxious to hurry on the last protracted moments of his dying benefactor.

This empire, totally unknown two centuries ago, has suddenly burst in upon the world, as if by sheer force, and with no invitation, with no real right, has taken its place at the council table of the sovereigns of Europe, and has peremptorily demanded its share of the booty, although this was won without its assistance.

No one has yet dared oppose its claims to interfere in the affairs of Europe.

Charles XII tried to do so; his sword, till then invincible, shivered in the attempt. Frederick II wanted to oppose the encroachments of the Petersburg Court; Königsberg and Berlin fell before the might of the Northern foe. The Emperor Napoleon penetrated to the very heart of this giant, at the head of half a million men—and escaped as best he could, alone, on a broken down common sledge. Europe looked on with amazement at Napoleon's flight, at the Cossack hosts hot on his trail, at the Russian armies marching towards Paris, bestowing national independence on Germany as though they were scattering alms by the wayside. Like a monstrous vampire, Russia seems to exist only in order to fasten on the mistakes of nations and their kings. Yesterday we saw her all but destroy Austria by way of helping her against Hungary: to-day we may see her proclaim the Mark of Brandenburg a province of the Russian Empire while professing to be the protector of the King of Prussia.

And yet on the very eve of the great struggle, how little we know about this new adversary—this arrogant nation, armed to the teeth, ready to march across the frontier at the slightest gesture from its confederates in reaction. We scarcely know what arms it carries, or the colour of its flag—and we rest content with official statements, with vague, current notions, barely noticing how much the various accounts we hear contradict one another.

From some we hear only of the omnipotence of the Tsar, of the arrogance of the government, of the cringing servility of the people: while others tell us that the despotism of St Petersburg is not a part of the national life, that the people, bent double under the twin yoke of the Emperor and the aristocracy, endure oppression without accepting it, suffer but are not broken—and all the while provide the cement that keeps together the vast Colossus that bestrides them. Some there are who say that the Russian people are a disgusting rabble of drunkards and helots, and there are others who say that Russia is the home of an intelligent and gifted race.

There is to me something tragic about the senile, hopeless fashion in which the old world runs together all these various views about its enemy.

In this whole vast farrago of incompatible opinions, there is so much evidence of tragic frivolity, of deeply embedded prejudice, of real failure to adapt oneself, that if we look for a parallel in history, our thoughts, whether we like it or not, inevitably turn to the decadence of Rome.

For it was in just this way that people in those days, on the very eve of the Christian revolution, on the very eve of the victory of barbarism, used to speak of Rome as immortal, and of the Nazarene sect as a negligible lunatic element, and ridiculed the dangers to which the unrest in the barbarian world should have made them alive.

Sir, you have the distinction of being the first person in France to have spoken of the Russian people. You put your hand on the very heart, on the very source of life. And it seemed as if the truth was about to be disclosed to you, had you not, in a sudden access of rage, pulled back the hand you had stretched out in friendship, and straightway the source seemed to run clouded and muddy.

With real distress I read your words of anger. It was with a heavy heart that I looked through them—and looked in vain—for the historian, for the philosopher, above all for that man of goodwill so familiar to us all. Let me hasten to add that I fully understand the cause of your indignation: it was sympathy for the misfortunes of Poland that prompted you to speak as you did. For sympathy with our Polish brothers is a feeling that we also know well, save that with us it is an occasion not merely for compassion but for remorse and shame. You talk about loving Poland? Surely we all love her, but can we not do so without having to persecute some other country no less wretched in its fate—and persecute it merely because it was press-ganged into serving its tyrannical government in a career of crime? Let us be generous. Let us not forget that only recently we were offered the spectacle of a country that boasts of universal suffrage and a citizen army, none the less prepared to help in the maintenance of ORDER from Warsaw to Rome. . . . Look at what has been going on under your very eyes . . . and yet we don't say that the French are no longer human. We are more patient.

It is time to forget this unhappy fratricidal strife. Neither side can emerge from it victorious. Both Russia and Poland go down before a common enemy. The martyrs, the victims themselves, turn their back upon the past finding it no less painful than we do. Your distinguished friend whom you quote, the great poet Mickiewicz, is proof of this.

I beg you, Sir, not to speak of the views of this Polish poet as displaying 'clemency, the faults of the saints.' No: they are rather the fruits of long and careful thought, of a deep insight into the destiny of the Slav world. It is noble to forgive one's enemies, but there is something still worthier of mankind: and that is to understand them, because to understand is necessarily to forgive, to justify, to reconcile.

The Slav world is moving towards unity: a tendency which became evident immediately after the Napoleonic period. The idea of a Slav federation is already explicit in the revolutionary plans of Pestel and Mouraviev.[1] Several Poles actually took part in the Russian conspiracy.

When the revolution of 1830 broke out in Warsaw, the Russian people showed no animosity whatever towards those who had rebelled against the Tsar. The young were heart and soul with the Polish cause. I can remember the enthusiasm with which we seized upon the news from Warsaw: we wept like children as we read about the famous memorial service celebrated in the Polish capital in commemoration of our Petersburg martyrs.[2] Any sympathy expressed for the Poles ran us the risk of the most appalling punishments, and so we had to conceal it in our hearts and remain silent.

It is possible that at the time of the war of 1830 the dominant sentiments in Poland were still a violent hatred—a sentiment entirely justified—and an exclusive form of nationalism. Since then, Mickiewicz, the various philo-

[1]Leaders of the abortive Decembrist revolt in 1825. Both were executed by Nicholas I in 1826.

[2]i.e. the Decembrists.

logical and historical studies produced by Slav writers, a deeper acquaintance with other European people acquired in the course of long wanderings in exile, have worked together to give a very different turn to Polish thought. The Poles have come to feel that the battle is not between them and the Russian people: they have learnt that they cannot fight otherwise than FOR THEIR FREEDOM AND OURS—to quote the solemn words inscribed on their revolutionary flag.

The heroic emissary Konarski, who was tortured and shot in Vilna in 1839, ignored all differences of nationality when he called on Russians and Poles alike to rise in revolt. Russia showed her gratitude in a way that was at once tragic and yet typical of everything that she has done since that day when she first came under the heel of the German jackboot.

An enthusiastic, passionate, fanatical young man, by the name of Koravaev, a Russian officer in the regiment garrisoning the fortress, decided to rescue Konarski. The day when he would be on duty came round. All the arrangements necessary for an escape had been made, when he was betrayed by one of those who had been accused at the same time as the Polish martyr, and the whole plan had to be abandoned. The young man was arrested: he was put in chains and sent to the mines of Siberia, there to expiate his crime, the crime of having obeyed a call higher than military orders. Nothing has been heard of him since.

I spent five years in exile in the remote provinces of the Russian Empire. There I had the opportunity of meeting a considerable number of Polish exiles, for in every district town one comes across them, either surrounded by their complete families or else leading wretched, solitary lives. I should very much like to call them as witnesses in my cause. Several of them have in the meanwhile returned to their homes. They would all—I am quite sure—speak of the abundant sympathy that they received from the local inhabitants. I am not, of course, talking here of the police or of the upper military hierarchy. This latter class is nowhere remarkable for its love of liberty, and least of all in Russia. Or again I could quote for your benefit those Polish students who every year are sent off to universities in Russia in order to keep them well away from Polish schools. I should like them to describe for themselves the welcome that they everywhere received from their new colleagues. They used to leave us with tears in their eyes.

You may remember, Sir, that in Paris in 1847 when the Polish émigrés were celebrating the anniversary of their revolution, a Russian appeared on the platform to appeal for friendship and beg that the past should be forgotten. That was our unhappy friend Michael Bakunin. But I do not want to quote only the example of one of my fellow countrymen. I want to appeal to one of those who are thought to be our enemies, a man whom you yourself mentioned in your fine epic about Kosciusko. Ask the Nestor of Polish democracy what he thinks on this subject, ask M. Biernacki, one of the ministers of revolutionary Poland, for his views. I will abide by the verdict of this noble intellect, although long periods of unhappiness might well have embittered him against anything connected with the name of Russia. He will not belie me.

The solidarity that binds Poland and Russia to one another and thence to the whole Slav world, cannot be denied: it stands out so clearly. I can go further: without Russia the Slav world has no future: without Russia, it will wither away, it will miscarry, it will be swallowed up by the German element, it will become Austria, it will fail to be itself. But I cannot believe that this in fact is to be its mission, its fate.

I must confess, Sir, that in studying the exposition of your ideas, I find I am quite unable to accept the argument whereby you try to prove that Europe as a whole is one living person, of which each nation is an indispensable organ.

It seems to me that all the Romano-German nations are necessary to the European world because they exist: but it would be difficult to prove that they exist because they are necessary. Aristotle made the distinction between pre-existing necessity and *a posteriori* necessity. Nature accepts the inevitability of existent facts: but, for all that, there is a great deal of change and variety within what is as yet unrealized and is still to be. It is then only on this principle that the Slav world can claim its unity—a claim strengthened by the fact that it consists entirely of one race.

Centralization is contrary to the Slav genius; federalism, on the other hand, is its natural form of expression. Once the Slav world has become unified, and knit together into an association of free autonomous peoples, it will at last be able to enter on its true historical existence. Its past can be seen only as a period of preparation, of growth, of purification. The historic forms of the State have never answered to the national ideal of the Slavs, an ideal which is vague, instinctive if you like, yet by the same token gives promise for the future of a truly remarkable vitality. In all their actions, the Slavs have always revealed a strange sort of detachment, a curious kind of apathy. So for instance we have the case of Russia changing as a whole from idolatry to Christianity, without any repercussion, without any revolution, simply out of passive obedience to the Grand Prince Vladimir and out of deference to Kiev. Without any regrets, people flung their old idols into the Volkhov and submitted to the new God as though it were a new idol.

Five hundred years later, a part of Russia accepted in just the same manner a civilization that had been ordered from abroad and bore upon it a German trademark.

The Slav world is like a woman who has never loved and so seems indifferent to all that goes on around her: listless, detached, remote. But we cannot tell what will happen in the future: the woman is young, and even now something seems to be stirring within her, making her heart beat faster.

If what is at stake is the richness of the national genius, we only need point to Poland—the only Slav country so far to enjoy freedom and power at the same moment.

The Slav world is not the heterogeneous affair it seems to be. Underneath the veneer of aristocratic, liberal, catholic Poland, of monarchic, oppressed, Byzantine Russia, underneath the democratic system of the Serb Voyevod and the Austrian bureaucracy that oppresses Illyria, Dalmatia and the Banat, underneath the patriarchal régime of the Osmanlis and the holy rule of the Archbishop of Montenegro, there is one single race, physiologically and ethnographically homogeneous.

The majority of the Slav peoples have never been subjugated by a conquering race. For them submission has, on the whole, been confined to the recognition of an overlord and to the payment of some form of tribute. Such, for instance, was the Mongol rule in Russia. As a result, the Slavs have managed to preserve for some hundreds of years their nationality, their way of life and their language.

The great question then is this: Is it reasonable to expect that Russia will be the nucleus of this crystallization, the centre towards which the Slav world will gravitate? a question we should ask realizing that so far she is the only section of that great race to be even provisionally organized into a State; and that there she stands, powerful, independent, armed with two swords, the one pointed against Germany, the other threatening Turkey. There could be no doubt at all about the answer to this question, if the Petersburg government had the faintest inkling of its national vocation, if any humane idea of any sort whatever could even once penetrate that gloomy and dull-witted despotism. But, as things are, how can anyone of any integrity or decency dare suggest to the western Slavs that they should ally themselves with an empire which lives in a permanent state of siege and where the sceptre is wielded like a truncheon in the hands of a flogging corporal.

The idea of a union based on the principles of freedom must not be confused with Imperial Panslavism, as it has been expounded in the past by misguided or corrupted men.

At this point, logic compels us to raise what is really the most serious, the most genuine question of all:

If we suppose that the Slav world has prospects of some more developed form of life in the future, then, which of all its somewhat embryonic elements is the most advanced, which gives the best ground for such hopes? If the Slavs are right in believing that their hour has come, then this element must necessarily be that which is in line with revolutionary ideas in Europe.

You have suggested which this element might be, you have touched upon it, but then you let it elude your grasp while you brushed away a tear of compassion for the fate of Poland.

You maintain that 'the basis of the life of the Russian people is COMMUNISM': you assert that 'its strength is founded on a form of agrarian law, on perpetual sub-division of the land.'

What a terrible MENE TEKEL have you pronounced.... Communism as a basis of life! Sub-division of the land as a source of strength! How is it, Sir, that you were not frightened by your own words?

Should we not pause here for reflection, and not leave the question until we have convinced you whether this is in fact the truth or whether it is pure fantasy?

As though there were any other real subjects of inquiry, any other serious questions for the nineteenth century than this question of communism and land division!

Carried away by indignation, you proceed: 'What they (the Russians) lack is that essential human attribute, the moral faculty, the sense of right and wrong. Truth and justice mean nothing to them. Mention these words to them—and they are mute, they smile at you, they don't understand what you are talking about.' Who are these Russians with whom you have spoken? And what notions of Justice and Truth are they that the Russians cannot understand? For in a genuinely revolutionary age, it is not enough simply to mention the words *truth* and *justice*. For these words no longer need have a meaning that is fixed and unambiguous for all of us alike.

The Justice and Truth of the old Europe are the injustice and falsehood of the Europe that is being born.

Nations are products of Nature: History is merely a progressive continuation of animal development. We shall get no nearer the truth as long as we consider Nature from the point of view of praise or blame. She has no time either for a Montyon prize or for our condemnations. Such moral categories do not apply to her: they are too subjective. It seems to me that a whole nation as such cannot be either completely good or totally bad: a nation is always true: there is no such thing as a nation that is a lie. All that Nature can do is to bring into existence that which is practically possible under certain given conditions: and then once it exists, to foster its growth by means of that divine ferment, that creative restlessness, that insatiable thirst, that need for self-fulfilment—the endless desire that exists in all living creatures.

Some peoples contrive to have a pre-historic, others an unhistoric, existence: but *once they have entered* the great stream of History, which is one and indivisible, all alike belong to humanity and, conversely, the whole of humanity's past belongs to them. In universal history—which is in fact humanity viewed in its progressive and active aspect—an aristocracy based on facial features, an aristocracy based on skin gradually become extinct. Anything that is not human has no part to play in history and consequently we never find there either a whole people entirely on the level of the herd or a whole people entirely elect.

No one nowadays could be so blind or so ungrateful as not to recognize the enormously important rôle that France plays in the fate of Europe: but, Sir, I must confess that I find it impossible to say, as you do, that France is a necessary condition, is a *sine qua non* of the march of history.

Nature never stakes her all on a single card. Rome, the Eternal City, which at one time could make a fair claim to be the ruler of the world, sank into decline, disintegrated, became extinct, and Humanity in its inhumanity moved on.

On the other hand, short of accusing Nature of absurdity and madness, I should find it difficult to see nothing but an outcast race, a lie, a mere conglomeration of creatures lower than mankind but with all the vices of mankind, in a nation which has a thousand formative years to its credit, which has with a rare obstinacy preserved its national integrity, which has welded itself into an empire, and which has affected the course of history—more so perhaps than it should have.

And such a view becomes even more unplausible when one realizes that this country, on its enemies' own admission, is anything but static. It is not a country, like China, that having attained some form of social organization more or less suited to its requirements, has sunk into a heavy sleep, into a condition of *semper idem*: even less is it a country, like that of the Hindus, that has outlived its strength and is now dying of senile decay. On the contrary, Russia is an Empire still in its youth; a building that still has about it the smell of fresh plaster, where everything is experimental and in a state of transition, where nothing is final, where people are always making changes, many of which are for the worse but all of which are at least changes. Such, in brief, is the people that, according to you, is based on Communism, that draws its strength from the sub-division of land.

After all, Sir, why do you reproach the Russian people? What is the real substance of your accusation?

'The Russian', you say, 'is a liar and a thief: he is a habitual liar and a habitual thief: and is so innocently, for it is in his nature to be so.'

Sir, I will not here comment on the excessive generality of this observation, but I should like to put to you, if I may, this simple question: Who in such cases is the victim, whom does the Russian lie to, and whom does he steal from? And the answer surely is that it is the landowner, the official, the civil servant, the judge, the police officer—in other words, the sworn enemies of the peasant, men whom he has come to look upon as Germanized apostates and traitors. Deprived of all means of self-protection, he tries to trick his oppressors, to deceive them, and, in doing so, is surely right. Cunning, a great thinker has said, is the irony of brute force.[1]

The Russian peasant who has, as you have rightly observed, a strong aversion to every form of landed property, who is improvident and indolent by temperament, has gradually and imperceptibly found himself caught up in the tentacles of the German bureaucracy and the feudal power. He has submitted to this degrading yoke with, I agree, the passivity of despair, but he has never believed either in the authority of his lord, or in the justice of the courts, or in the equity of the administration. For almost two hundred years, his whole life has been one long, dumb, passive opposition to the existing order of things: he has endured oppression, he has groaned under it: but he has never accepted anything that goes on outside the life of the rural commune.

The idea of the Tsar still enjoys some considerable prestige in the mind of the peasant. But it is not the actual Tsar Nicholas whom he adores, it is rather an abstract idea,

[1] *Biography of Hegel* by Rosenkranz (Posthumous works).—A.H.

a myth, a kind of Providence, an Avenger of evils, an embodiment of justice in the popular imagination.

Apart from the Tsar, only the Clergy are capable of having any moral influence on Orthodox Russia. The higher clergy are the sole representatives of ancient Russia within the administration. The clergy have never shaved off their beards, and through this very fact have remained on the side of the people. The people have complete faith in anything they are told by a monk. However, the monks and the higher clergy, for all their talk about being dedicated to matters not of this world, are almost entirely indifferent to the people. The village priest has lost all influence on account of his greed, his drunkenness, and his close association with the police. Here again, it is not the man but the idea that the people respect.

As for the Dissenters, they hate both the Tsar and the village priest, both the man and the idea.

Apart from the Tsar and the Clergy, all the other elements within society and the administration are utterly alien and ultimately hostile to the people. The peasant is, quite literally, outside the law: the law contrives to offer him absolutely no protection whatsoever, and his only share in the existing order of things is confined to the payment of the double tribute which grinds him down: the tribute of blood and the tribute of sweat. So, spurned on all sides, he comes to feel that the government is not for him but against him, that the single aim of the administration and the nobility is to extort from him as much work and as much money as possible. Realizing this and blessed with a certain shrewd, cunning intelligence he manages to deceive all of them all the time. Nor could he very well do anything else, because if he told them the truth, that would be an admission, an acceptance on his part of their power: if he didn't steal from them (and notice that he is accused of stealing when he conceals any part of the produce of his own labour), if he didn't steal from them, then this would be a recognition on his part—and a quite fatal one—of the propriety of these exactions, of the rights of the landowners and of the fairness of his judges.

In order to appreciate the real position of the Russian peasant, you need to see him before one of these courts of law: you have only to see for yourself the sad, frightened eyes, the sullen set of the jaw, the anxious searching look he turns on all around him, to realize that his position is no better than that of a captured rebel brought before a court martial, or that of a traveller facing a gang of brigands. From the first glance, it is quite clear that the victim has no trust in these cruel, hostile, implacable creatures who interrogate him and torture him and finally mulct him dry. He knows that if he has any money, then he will be acquitted, and if he hasn't, he will be condemned without mercy.

When he speaks, he uses a somewhat antiquated Russian: whereas the judge and his clerks use the modern bureaucratic language which is so garbled an affair as to be barely intelligible. First they fill whole folios with their ungrammatical solecisms, and then they reel it off at the peasant in a high nasal twang as fast as they can go. What he hears is an undifferentiated flux of noise, of which he must, if he is to preserve his skin, make such sense as he can. He is fully aware of what is at issue, and is on his guard. He is sparing in his use of words, tries hard to cover up his nervousness, and the result is that he stands there with an asinine look on his face, like a great booby, like someone who has lost the power of speech.

He leaves the court in the same wretched state whether he has been condemned or whether he has been acquitted. The difference between the two verdicts seems to him a matter of mere chance or luck.

In much the same way, when he is summoned as a witness, he insists on perjuring himself, on knowing nothing, on denying everything, even when the evidence on the other side is overwhelming. In the eyes of the Russian people, there is no stigma attached to a man merely because he has been found guilty in a court of law. Convicts and those who are sentenced to transportation are in popular parlance called '*unfortunates*'.

The Russian peasant has no real knowledge of any form of life but that of the village commune: he understands about rights and duties only when these are tied to the commune and its members. Outside the commune, there are no obligations for him—there is simply violence. The fatal element in his character is that he submits to the violence, not that, in his own way, he denies it and tries to protect himself by guile. It is far more honest to lie before a judge whom one doesn't acknowledge, than to make some show of respect for a jury packed by the police, whose monstrous corruption is as clear as daylight. The peasant respects his institutions only in so far as he finds embodied there his own notions of Right and Justice.

There is one fact that has never been denied by anyone who has any real first-hand knowledge of the Russian people. And that is that they very rarely cheat one another. An almost boundless good faith prevails amongst them: contracts and written agreements are quite unheard of.

Problems connected with surveying are necessarily extremely complicated on account of the perpetual subdivision of the land according to the number of people working on it.[1] And yet the peace of the Russian countryside is never disturbed by any complaints or litigation. The government and the landowners ask for nothing better than some pretext for interference, but none is ever afforded them. The petty differences that arise are quickly settled either by the elders or by the commune: everyone abides by such decisions without reservation. The same thing happens in the nomadic communes of artisans (the *artel*).

[1] And not according to the number of children.—A.H.

There are a number of such *artels*—builders, carpenters and other sorts of artisans—each consisting of several hundred people drawn from different communes, who come together for a given period of time, for a year for instance, and so form a group. When the year is up, the workers share out the produce on the basis of the work they have done, in each case abiding by the general decision. The police have not so far had the satisfaction of being able to interfere in these arrangements. The association, I must emphasize, generally holds itself responsible for all the workers who comprise it.

The bonds between peasants of the same commune are much closer when the commune is not Orthodox but Dissenter. From time to time the government organizes a savage raid on one of these Dissenting communes. The whole population is imprisoned and then deported, without any preconceived plan, without any repercussions, without any provocation, without any necessity, merely in compliance with the instructions of the clergy or the depositions of the police. It is in the course of these persecutions of Dissenters, that one can see the Russian peasant as he really is and observe the solidarity that ties him to his fellows. One can see him on such occasions tricking the police, rescuing his fellow believers, hiding the holy books and vessels, undergoing the most appalling tortures without uttering a word. I challenge anyone to produce a single example of a Dissenting commune that has been betrayed by a peasant, even an Orthodox.

This trait in the ordinary Russian makes all police inquiries extremely difficult to carry out. And I heartily congratulate him on it. The Russian peasant has no other morality than that which flows quite instinctively and naturally from his communal life: it is profoundly national in character and the little that he knows about the Gospels fortifies him in it: the shocking corruption of the government and of the landlords binds him ever more closely to his traditional customs and to his commune.[1] The commune has preserved the Russian people from Mongol

[1]The peasants on one of the communes belonging to Prince Kozlovsky, bought their freedom at a price agreed upon with the landowner. The land was then divided up between the peasants in accordance with the amount of money that each had contributed to the fund that had bought them their liberty. This arrangement seemed to be one that was as fair as it was natural. However, the peasants found it so awkward and so little in accord with their ordinary way of life, that they decided to make themselves jointly responsible for the purchase money and regard it simply as a debt incurred by the commune as a whole, and to proceed with the division of the land on what was for them the normal system. The authority for this is Haxthausen who recounts it in his *Études sur la vie populaire en Russie*. The author visited the commune in question personally.

M. Tengoborski, a member of the Russian Council of State, in a book recently published in Paris and bearing a dedication to the Emperor Nicholas, says that the system of land-division seems to him unfavourable to agricultural development (as though agriculture had to be favourable to agricultural development!), but he adds: 'It would be very difficult to obviate these disadvantages, because the system of land division is bound up with the organization of the communes which *it would be dangerous to touch*: it rests on the fundamental notion of the unity of the commune and the equal right of every member of it to a share in the communal land. In this way, it reinforces and strengthens the communal spirit which is one of the stablest elements in the social organization. It is at the same time one of the best bulwarks against the increase of the proletariat and communist ideas.' (It is easy to realize that a people already enjoying the practice of the commune has nothing to fear from communist ideas.) 'What is remarkable is the good sense and the efficiency with which the peasants, generally without any external assistance, modify the inconvenient features of the system to suit local conditions, and the readiness with which they make adjustments to offset any inequality of distribution arising out of the quality of the soil itself, and the confidence with which they submit to adjudication by the elders of the commune. One might easily imagine that these land allocations, which have to be frequently revised, would give rise to innumerable disputes, and yet the parties involved seldom appeal to established authority. This fact, which is surprising in itself, can admit of only one explanation, and that is that the system, for all its potential defects, barbarism, from Imperial civilization, from the Europeanized landowners and from the German bureaucracy: the organic life of the commune has persisted despite all the attempts made on it by authority, badly mauled though it has been at times. By good fortune it has survived right into the period that witnesses the rise of Socialism in Europe.

For Russia this has been a most happy providence.

The Russian aristocracy is entering on a new phase of its existence. Born of an anti-national revolution, it has accomplished its appointed task. It has brought into being a vast empire, a large army, and a centralized government. Devoid of all principles and traditions, it has nothing further to do. It has, it is true, arrogated to itself another task, that of importing Western civilization into Russia, and it had some measure of success in doing this so long as it played the part of being a civilized governing class.

This part it has now abandoned.

The government which originally cut itself off from the people in the name of civilization, has now, a hundred years later, hurriedly cut itself off from civilization in the name of absolutism.

This happened as soon as it detected the tricolour of liberalism dimly visible, like a spectre, through the tendencies of civilization. It then tried to fall back on the idea of nationalism and on the people. But this was impossible: there was by now no common ground between the people and the government—the people had grown completely away from the government, and the government in turn seemed to see in the masses something even more

has become so much identified with the way of life and habits of the people that they put up with its drawbacks without a murmur.'

'The notion of association'—says the same author—'is as natural to the Russian peasant and as integral to all aspects of his life, as the notion of corporation, the municipal idea, which is central to the bourgeoisie of the West, is in conflict with his habits and outlook.' *Études sur les forces productives de la Russie*, by M. Tengoborski, vol. I, p. 331 and p. 142.—A.H.

terrifying than anything it knew—the Red Spectre. All things considered, liberalism seemed to be less dangerous than the prospect of a new Pugachev.[1] But the horror and the disgust in which all liberal ideas were held had now become such that the government could no longer make its peace with civilization.

From then onwards, the sole aim of Tsarism has been Tsarism, ruling for ruling's sake. Immense new forces have been called into being, each one of them at once supplementing and neutralizing all the others, so that in this way a quite artificial stability has been attained.

But autocracy for autocracy's sake is ultimately an impossibility: it is too pointless, too sterile.

This has now been realized, and so some sort of outlet has been looked for in Europe. Russian diplomacy is feverishly active: there is a constant despatch of notes, agents, suggestions, threats, promises, spies. The Emperor sees himself as the natural protector of all German princes. He dabbles in every petty intrigue in every petty court. He settles all their little differences, bestowing on one a reprimand, on another a Grand Duchess. But even this doesn't exhaust his energy. He has become the policeman of the whole world, the prop of all forms of reaction and all forms of barbarism. He sets himself up as the supreme representative of the monarchical principle in Europe, giving himself the airs of an aristocrat, as though he were a Bourbon or a Tudor and had for his courtiers Devonshires, or, at the very lowest, Montmorencys.

The sad part of this is that there really is nothing in common between feudal monarchy with its avowed principles, its roots in the past, its social and religious ideology, and the Napoleonic despotism of St Petersburg, which has no principles behind it, and is based entirely on grim historic necessity and some passing need that it satisfies.

[1]Leader of a cossack peasant revolt in the 18th century.

And gradually the Winter Palace, like a mountain peak at the end of the warm season, becomes covered over with layer upon layer of snow and ice. The sap, which was artificially induced to rise into these elevated social reaches, now slowly recedes from them, so that all they can now command is a certain brute strength, a mere physical hardness like that of a rock good for a while longer against the waves of revolution which break idly at its base.

Surrounded by his generals and his ministers and his officers and his bureaucrats, Nicholas defies his isolation, but visibly he grows gloomier: he becomes morose, preoccupied. He realizes that no one has any affection for him, he senses the gloomy silence that surrounds him, through which he can hear only too well the distant rumblings that seem to draw closer. The Tsar tries to forget all this, and announces to the world that his sole concern is the aggrandizement of the Imperial power.

Such declarations are nothing new: for the last twenty-five years he has toiled unremittingly, without respite, for this cause and this alone: in pursuit of it he has spared nothing, neither tears nor blood.

Everything that he has undertaken has prospered: he has crushed Polish nationalism, and in Russia he has extinguished liberalism.

What more can he want? Why is he so depressed?

The Emperor knows that Poland is not really dead. And in place of the liberalism that he has persecuted with such gratuitous savagery for that exotic flower could never have taken root in Russian soil, being quite alien to the national character—he now sees another problem lowering like a storm cloud.

The people are beginning to murmur and grow restless under the yoke of the nobility: small revolts break out all the time: you yourself, Sir, have referred to one terrible instance of this.

The party of movement, of progress, demands the

emancipation of the peasants; and its members are ready to set an example by sacrificing their own rights. The Tsar is in a state of permanent indecision, and has lost the power of all real thought: he wants emancipation, and yet does all he can to prevent it.

He has come to see that the emancipation of the peasant is tantamount to the emancipation of the land: and that the emancipation of the land would in turn usher in a social revolution and would make rural communism sacrosanct. To evade this question of emancipation is certainly impossible: to postpone it until the reign of his successor would be easier but cowardly, and the time gained would really be no better than time spent in a wretched posting-station waiting for fresh horses.

From all this you can see what a blessing it is for Russia that the rural commune has never been broken up, that private ownership has never replaced the property of the commune: how fortunate it is for the Russian people that they have remained outside all political movements, and, for that matter, outside European civilization, which would undoubtedly have sapped the life of the commune, and which to-day in Socialism has achieved its own negation.

Europe, as I have pointed out elsewhere, has never solved the antinomy of the State and the individual, but it has stated the problem. Russia approaches the same problem from a quite different direction, but it has had no greater success in finding a solution to it. It is then in the shadow of this problem that we find the source of our equality.

Europe, now on the point of taking the first step forward in a social revolution, is confronted by a country that can provide an actual instance of an attempt—a crude, barbaric attempt perhaps, but still an attempt of a sort—in the direction of the division of the land amongst those who work it. And observe that this lesson is provided not by civilized Russia but by the people themselves in their daily lives. We Russians who have absorbed European civilization cannot hope to be more than a means to an end—the yeast in the leavening—a bridge between the Russian people and revolutionary Europe. The future of Russia lies with the *moujik*, just as the regeneration of France lies with the worker.

But if this is so, then surely the Russian people have some claim on your indulgence? Surely, Sir, this is so.

Poor peasant! So intelligent, so simple in his habits, so easily satisfied, he has been seized on as the butt of every vicious attack. The Emperor decimates his number by conscription: the landowner steals every third day of his working week: the *tchinovnik*[1] worms out of him his last rouble. The peasant suffers all in silence, but without despair. He holds hard to his commune. If someone tears a limb off it, it heals over, it comes together all the more. The fate of the poor peasant surely deserves pity, and yet he receives none: instead of commiseration, he is showered with abuse.

You, Sir, deny the last refuge that is open to him, the one place left where he can still feel himself to be a man, where he can know love and not fear. For you say that 'his commune is not really a commune, his family is not really a family, his wife is not really his wife: before she belongs to him, she belongs to his lord; his children are not really his children, and who knows who is their father?'

In this style you hold up this unfortunate people not to scientific scrutiny but to the scorn of the whole world, which will read and accept and admire all these fine stories that you give them.

It is then my duty to say something on the subject.

The family is something very highly developed amongst all the Slav races: it is possibly here that we have the source of their conservatism, the limit of their negative tendency.

The prototype of the commune is the family owning all things in common.

[1] i.e. the government official.

Amongst these rural families, there is no desire to split up into different households, and so one often finds three or four generations living together under one roof and ruled over in a patriarchal manner either by the grandfather or by a great-uncle. Women, for the most part, lead a rather oppressed life, as is generally the case in an agricultural community, but in Russia they are treated with respect when their sons come of age and even more so if they are the widows of family chiefs.

It is by no means uncommon to find the conduct of affairs entirely in the hands of a grey-haired grandmother. Can it, then, really be said that the family doesn't exist in Russia?

Now let us turn to the relations that exist between the landowner and his serf families.

But if we are to have a clear picture of the situation, we must first distinguish between the law and the abuses of the law, between what is permitted and what is criminal.

The *droit du seigneur* has never existed among the Slav peoples.

The landowner has no legal right to demand either the first joys of marriage or any subsequent infidelity. If the law were properly enforced in Russia, then the seduction of a serf would be punished in exactly the same way as an offence against a free woman: that is to say, it would make the offender liable either to penal servitude or to exile in Siberia according to the gravity of the actual offence. So much for the law: now let us look at the facts.

It is undeniable that with the social position that the aristocracy are allowed by the Government, it is very easy for them to seduce the wives and daughters of their serfs. The landowner, with his powers of confiscation and punishment, can always find husbands willing to hand over their wives, and fathers ready to dispose of their daughters —rather like that splendid French nobleman in the middle of the eighteenth century who, according to Peuchot's

Mémoires, begged for the special privilege of being allowed to install his daughter in the Parc-aux-Cerfs.

It is scarcely surprising that honest fathers and husbands can obtain no redress against the nobility, thanks to the excellent judiciary in Russia. They find themselves in a position much like that of Monsieur Tiercelin whose daughter of eleven was abducted by Berryer with the connivance of Louis XV. I do not deny that such disgusting abuses are perfectly possible—indeed one has only to think of the crude and depraved habits of one section of the Russian nobility to realize it. But this does not mean that the peasants are indifferent spectators of their masters' debauchery: far from it.

Let me produce some evidence for this.

Half the landowners who are murdered by their peasants and statistics show that the total is between sixty and seventy a year) are killed in revenge for their erotic exploits. The peasant very seldom brings an action against his master because he knows that the court will completely disregard his grievances. But he has his axe, in the use of which he is a real master, and he knows it.

So much for the peasantry: and now, Sir, I beg you to bear with me for a little in what I have to say about civilized Russia.

Our intellectual movement has fared no better at your hands than our national character: with a single stroke of the pen you dismissed everything that we have ever done, all the work of our fettered hands.

One of Shakespeare's characters, at a loss for some way to humiliate an opponent he despises, exclaims: 'I even doubt your existence.' You have gone further, Sir: you don't doubt the non-existence of Russian literature.

I quote your very words:

'I cannot attach any real importance to the efforts of a few clever people in St Petersburg, who have experimented a little with the Russian language rather as if it were a learned language and have deceived Europe with a wan travesty of a national literature. If it were not for my deep respect for Mickiewicz and his saintly aberrations, I really should blame him for the charity, one might almost say the indulgence, with which he speaks of this frippery.'

I am quite unable, Sir, to find any reason for the scornful way in which you receive the first agonized cry of a people awakening in its prison-house, a movement which the gaoler tries to stifle at birth.

Why have you been so unwilling to listen to the heart-rending accents of our sad poetry, of our songs which are merely tears given tongue? What is it that has warped your understanding of the nervous, hysterical laughter in our literature, of the unfailing irony which conceals the deep wound in our heart, and which is, in the last analysis, the terrible confession of our utter impotence?

How I wish I could translate for you adequately some of the lyrical poems of Pushkin, or Lermontov, or some of Koltsov's ballads! Then you would welcome us with open arms, you would be the very first to beg us to forget everything you had said before.

Apart from the communal life of the *moujik*, there is nothing so characteristic of Russia, nothing that bodes so well for her future as her literary movement.

Between the peasant and literature there looms up the ghastly figure of official Russia, of 'the Russian lie, of the Russian cholera'—as you have so well named it.

This Russia starts with the Emperor and you can follow it right down from soldier to soldier, from clerk to clerk, until you come to the humblest official in a police-station in the farthest district of the Empire. In this way it ramifies indefinitely and at every stage—like the '*bolgi*' of Dante—it gains a new power for evil, it becomes even more depraved and tyrannical. So we have this living pyramid of crimes, abuses, impositions, floggings, the work of inhuman German officials everlastingly on the make, of illiterate judges everlastingly drunk, of aristocrats everlastingly toadying: the whole thing welded together by ties of common gain and common guilt, and in the last resort upheld by six hundred thousand automata armed with bayonets.

The peasant never defiles himself by any contact with the world of cynical officialdom: he suffers—that is the extent of his guilt.

The opposition to official Russia consists of a handful of desperate men who spend their lives in denouncing it, attacking it, unmasking it, sapping its strength.

From time to time one of these lone champions is dragged off to prison, tortured, deported to Siberia, but his place does not stay empty for long: fresh champions step into the breach. Such is our tradition, our inalienable inheritance.

The ghastly consequences that attend the spoken word in Russia inevitably increase its effectiveness. The voice of the free man is listened to with love and veneration, because in our country, it is raised only when there is something serious to say. The decision to put one's thoughts on paper is one not lightly made when at the foot of every page there looms up the prospect of a policeman, a *troika*, a *kibitka*, and in the distance Tobolsk or Irkoutsk.

In my last pamphlet, I wrote enough about Russian literature: here I shall only add a few general observations.

Sadness, scepticism, irony—these are the three strings of the Russian lyre.

When Pushkin begins one of his finest poems with these restrained, melancholy words:

> 'There is no justice on earth—nor any above us either.
> That is as clear to me as a simple musical scale.' [1]

[1] *Mozart and Salieri*. The poem has been quite perfectly translated into German, by M. Bornstaedt, in a little volume of translations from Pushkin and Lermontov.—A.H.

doesn't this chill your heart, don't you seem to see behind the apparent tranquillity a broken life, don't you detect a man who has become inured to suffering?

Lermontov, barely 30 years of age, filled with disgust at the society in which he finds himself, addresses one of his contemporaries in these words:

'I look on my generation with grief: its future is blank and grim: it will grow old in inaction, it will sink under the weight of doubt and barren science.

'Life exhausts us like a journey without a destination.

'We are like those ratheripes which are sometimes found, strange orphans amongst the blossom: they delight neither the eye nor the palate: they fall as they ripen. . . .

'We hurry towards the tomb, without happiness, without glory, and before we die we cast a look of bitter scorn over our past.

'We shall pass through this world unnoticed, a pensive, silent, soon forgotten company.

'We shall leave nothing to our descendants, no fruitful idea, no work of genius, and they will insult our remains with some contemptuous verse or with the sarcasm a destitute son might use to his spendthrift father.'

I know of only one other modern poet who has sounded the sombre notes of the human heart with the same intensity. He, too, was a poet born in slavery, and he likewise died before the rebirth of his native country. I mean that apologist of death, the famous Leopardi, he who saw the world as a vast league of criminals ruthlessly warring against a few virtuous madmen.

Russia has produced only one painter who is widely known: Brullov.[1] Where did this artist look for his inspiration? What is the subject of his masterpiece which won him something of a reputation in Italy?

[1]Karl Brullov (1799–1852), the first Russian painter to win an international reputation, was born in Italy, of Huguenot extraction

Look at this strange work.

Across an enormous canvas you see groups of terrified and bewildered people. Despite their efforts to escape, many are dying, the victims of an earthquake, of a volcanic eruption, of a truly cataclysmic storm. They are overwhelmed by some savage, senseless, evil force against which all struggle is unavailing. Such is the kind of inspiration that can be drawn from the atmosphere of Petersburg.

The Russian novel is entirely a study in pathological anatomy. It is one long diagnosis of the evil that consumes us, one sustained work of self-accusation, a pitiless, inexorable accusation. What we never hear is that gentle voice which comes down from Heaven, the voice that announced to Faust the forgiveness of the young, sinful girl. We must not look here for consolation, the only voices to be heard are those of doubt and damnation. And yet if Russia is to achieve salvation, it will be on account of this profound awareness that we have of our predicament, and the scant trouble we take to conceal it from the world.

He who frankly admits his failings, feels that he has something within him that will survive and overcome any disaster: he knows that he can redeem the past, and not only hold his head high but that, as in Byron's tragedy, he can

and came to Russia as a child. He studied in Rome, and his reputation was made entirely on the strength of *The Destruction of Pompeii* (1828–30). This picture was inspired by a visit to the ruins and influenced by Pliny's descriptions and Pacini's opera *L'ultimi giorni di Pompei* (1825). The enormous vogue that it enjoyed was due partly to its vast scale, partly to its eclectic combination of melodramatic lighting and reminiscences of Italian masters. Sir Walter Scott is said to have stood in front of it for an hour and declared it to be not a picture but an epic. It directly inspired Bulwer Lytton's novel. On his return to Russia, Brullov never repeated his early success, although some of his portraits are interesting studies. *The Destruction of Pompeii* now hangs in the Russian Museum, Leningrad.

turn from being 'Sardanapalus the profligate to Sardanapalus the hero.'

The Russian people do not read. Nor, of course, were Voltaire and Diderot read by villagers; they were read by the aristocracy and the Third Estate. In Russia the enlightened section of the Third Estate is part of the aristocracy, for the aristocracy nowadays includes everyone who is above the level of the people: it even includes an aristocratic proletariat which at one end merges into the people, and it includes a proletariat of freed men who work their way up the social scale and then become noble. This process of movement, this continual flux, gives the Russian aristocracy a character which you find nowhere else amongst the privileged classes of Europe. In short, all Russian history since Peter I is entirely the history of the aristocracy, and of the influence of European civilization upon it. Here I must mention that the size of the aristocracy in Russia is at least half that of the total number of electors in France, since the law of May 31st.[1]

During the eighteenth century, the most important theme in neo-Russian literature was the development of that rich, sonorous and magnificent language that we use to-day: a language which is at once supple and powerful, capable of expressing the most abstract notions of German metaphysics, and also the light, witty, sparkling phrases of French conversation. This literature, called into being by the genius of Peter the Great, bears, it is true, a sort of governmental imprint—but in those days being on the side of government meant being on the side of reform, almost on the side of revolution.

The Imperial throne was, right up to the great revolution of '89, majestically draped in the grandest robes of European civilization and philosophy. It was fitting that Catherine II

[1]French electoral law of May 31st, 1850, abolishing universal male suffrage and reducing register of voters from 10 million to 7 million.

should be entertained with villages [1] made out of cardboard and with wooden palaces with the distemper still fresh upon them: no one knew better than she the art of *mise-en-scène*. At the Hermitage Voltaire and Montesquieu and Beccaria vied with one another in displaying their talents. You know, Sir, the reverse of the medal.

Meanwhile, a strange, unexpected note began to break in on the triumphal choruses of pindaric odes to which the Court was given over. It was a note in which sarcastic irony, a tendency towards criticism and scepticism were apparent, and it was, I must say, the one truly national note to be heard, the only note sounded that had any real vitality in it, that gave any promise for the future. The others, transitory and exotic affairs, were doomed to perish.

The true character of Russian thought, whether in poetry or in speculation, emerges only in a fully developed, vital form after the accession of Nicholas. The distinctive traits of this movement, are a new and tragic sense of right and wrong, an implacable spirit of negation, a bitter irony, a tortured self-questioning. Sometimes a note of wild laughter accompanies it, but it is laughter without gaiety.

Living under these truly oppressive conditions, the Russian, who possesses an unclouded intelligence and a ruthlessly logical mind, soon emancipated himself from religion and traditional morality.

The emancipated Russian is the most independent creature in the world. And what indeed could there be to restrain him? A sense of the past? . . . But then isn't the starting point of modern Russia just the denial of tradition and national sentiment?

Or a sense of the past indefinite, the Petersburg period?

[1]Herzen is here referring to the famous Tauric expedition of Catherine II, January–June 1787, when the Empress made a ceremonial progress down the Dnieper to the Crimea: en route she was joined by Joseph II. Potemkin is said to have decorated the river banks with cardboard villages.

But that surely lays no obligation on us: 'this fifth act of a blood-stained drama, set in a brothel'[1] freed us from our old beliefs, but committed us to no new ones.

Your history, on the other hand, the history of the West, provides us with certain lessons, but no more: we do not consider ourselves the legal executors of your past.

We can share your scepticism—it is your faith that leaves us cold. You are too religious for us. We can share your animosities—it is your attachment to the legacy of the past that is incomprehensible to us. We are too oppressed, too wretched to make do with a mere half-liberty. You have your commitments to consider, your scruples to restrain you—but we have none of this, no commitments and no scruples—it is merely that for the moment we are powerless.

Here, Sir, is the source of that irony, of that rage that drives us to desperate measures, that takes possession of us and forces us on and on until it brings us to Siberia and the rack, to exile and early death. We have dedicated ourselves to a cause but without hope, in disgust and boredom. There is something truly irrational about our lives, but nothing that is either banal or stagnant or bourgeois.

Do not accuse us of being immoral merely because we do not respect the things that you respect. Would you condemn a foundling for having no respect for his parents? We are free agents, because we are self-made. The only element of tradition that we accept is that involved in our organic, our national way of life: and that is inherent in our very being: it is in our blood, it acts upon us more like an instinct than like some external authority to which we feel we must bend our wills. We are independent, because we possess nothing. There are literally no demands upon our affections. All our memories are tinged with bitterness and resentment. The fruits of civilization and learning were offered us at the end of the knout.

[1]As it has been admirably described by a writer in *Il Progresso*, in the course of an article on Russia, August 1st, 1851.—A.H.

What obligation, then, have we, the younger sons, the castaways of the family, to acknowledge any of your traditional duties? And how could we in all honesty accept this threadbare morality of yours, a morality which is neither humane nor Christian, which has no existence outside a few rhetorical exercises and speeches for the prosecution? How can you expect us to have any respect for the praetorium in which you administer your Barbaro-Roman justice, for those gloomy, oppressive vaults, where no light or air ever penetrates, rebuilt in the Middle Ages and then patched up by the enfranchised Third Estate? What goes on in them is possibly better than the robbery that goes on in the Russian courts, but could anyone maintain that it had anything to do with justice?

It is quite clear that any difference there may be between your laws and our Ukases lies almost entirely in the wording of their preambles. Ukases start with a painful truth—'The Tsar commands . . .'—whereas your laws start with an insulting lie, the triple Republican motto, the ironical invocation in the name of the French people. The *Code Nicholas* is intended to be unreservedly against mankind and in favour of authority. The *Code Napoléon* seems really no different. There are already enough impositions that we are forced to endure, without our making the position worse by imposing new ones on ourselves of our own free will. In this respect our situation is exactly like that of the peasantry. We bow to brute force: we are slaves because we have no way of freeing ourselves: but whatever happens, we shall accept nothing from the enemy camp.

Russia will never be Protestant.

Russia will never be *juste-milieu*.

Russia will never stage a revolution with the sole aim of ridding herself of Tsar Nicholas only to replace him by a multitude of other Tsars—Tsar-deputies, Tsar-tribunals, Tsar-policemen, Tsar-laws.

Possibly we ask too much, and shall achieve nothing.

That may be so, but we shall not despair. Before 1848, Russia neither should nor could have embarked on a career of revolution. At that time she had still much to learn—and she is learning it. Even the Tsar himself sees this: and this is the reason why he has made himself the scourge of the universities, of all speculation, of all learning. He is struggling hard to isolate Russia from the rest of the world and to stamp out all civilization: He is true to his profession —*il fait son métier*.

Will he succeed?

I have said elsewhere one must not put blind faith in the future; every foetus has the right to develop, but for all that not every foetus does develop. The future of Russia does not depend on herself alone: it is bound up with the future of Europe as a whole. Who can foretell what lies in store for the Slav world, should Reaction and Absolutism triumph over the European Revolution?

Perhaps it will perish—who knows?

But then Europe also will perish. . . .

And history will continue in America. . . .

I had written as far as this, Sir, when I received the last two pamphlets composing your epic. My first impulse on reading them was to throw what I had written on the fire. A man with your noble and generous heart did not need to wait for someone else to protest before according justice to a despised country. With your sympathy and kindness of heart, you couldn't keep up for long the rôle of the inexorable judge, of the avenger of a martyred race. You contradict yourself, but such contradictions are sublime.

However, when I reread my letter, it occurred to me that you might find there some observations about Russia and the Slav world that were new to you: so I decided to send it. I have complete confidence that you will pardon me for those passages where I allowed myself to be carried away by barbarian fury. It is not for nothing that Cossack blood flows in one's veins. I so longed to be able to change your opinions about the Russian people: it was so sad, so painful for me to see you treat us with such ruthlessness: I couldn't altogether suppress the grief that I felt and I let my pen run away with me. Now I see that you do not despair of us: I see that under the Russian peasant's coarse kaftan, you discover a human being, and now, for my part, I must confess to you that we perfectly understand what sort of picture the mere name of Russia conjures up in the mind of every free person. We have so often cursed our unhappy country ourselves. You know that well, Sir, else you would not have written those remarkable words—'Everything that we have said about the moral nullity of Russia is feeble in comparison with what Russians themselves have said about it.'

But, like you, we now feel that the time for these funeral orations on Russia is over and with you we say 'sous la tombe est une étincelle'[1]—'in the tomb—a spark of life'. You suspected it, guided by the insight of love: but we have seen it, we have experienced it. The spark of life has not been quenched, neither in the torrents of blood that have flowed, nor in the snows of Siberia, nor in the depths of mines and prisons. May it continue to smoulder under the ashes—for the cruel, bitter, icy wind that blows from Europe is strong enough to put it out. Russia finds herself hemmed in between two Siberias: the one white with snow, the other 'white' in its opinions.

For us the hour of action has not yet come. France can still rightly boast of having the honour of the van: all the difficulties of decision are still hers—and will be so even in 1852. It is obvious that Europe must take the lead—whether it be into the tomb or into a new life—and we shall follow

[1]cf. '. . . Si ta tombe est fermée
Laisse-moi, dans ta cendre un instant ranimée,
Trouver une étincelle. . . .'

A. de Musset: *Une Soirée Perdue*.

her not just because Europe is older than us but because there is this intimate link—as I have tried to bring home to you—between social revolution on the one hand and the fate of the Slav world on the other. The day of action may still be far off: the day of conscience, of thought, of speech has already dawned. We have lived long enough in sleep and silence: it is now time to tell of our dreams, to impart the fruit of our meditations.

Indeed, whose fault is it that the world had to wait until 1843, for the day 'when a German (Haxthausen) discovered' —that is the very word you use—'the Russia of the peasantry, of which until then people knew no more than they did of America before Christopher Columbus.'

It is our fault. It is the fault, I freely admit it, of our dumbness, of our cowardice, of the way we have allowed our tongues to be paralysed with fear, our imagination blighted by terror. Outside our frontiers we are even terrified of admitting how terrified we are of our chains. Born convicts, condemned to wear fetters until the day of our death, we feel insulted when people refer to us as willing slaves, as the negroes of the north, and yet we never think of openly disabusing them.

We must make up our minds whether we intend to endure these accusations, or whether we intend to put a stop to them and let free Russian speech be heard once again. It is far better to die under suspicion of being human than to bear the brand of slavery on one's forehead for ever, to live under the shameful reproach of being a slave by desire.

Unfortunately, in Russia, free speech is found shocking, terrifying. I tried to lift a small corner of the thick veil that hides us from the gaze of Europe: I confined myself to certain general intellectual tendencies, certain long-term aspirations, certain organic developments that the future holds in store: and yet, for all that, my pamphlet—about which you were kind enough to express yourself in such flattering terms—made a painful impression in Russia.

Friends, people whom I respect, raised their voices in condemnation. People accused it of being an admission of guilt. An admission . . . of what sort of crime? Of the crime of unhappiness, of suffering, of a desire to escape from our hateful position. . . . Poor, dear friends, forgive me this fault—for now I am falling into it again!

Ah, Sir, it is a hard and terrible thing to endure the yoke of slavery without being able to strike a blow, without any immediate hope of release. In the end it crushes even the best, the noblest, the most enthusiastic of men. Where is the hero who will not ultimately give way to weariness and despair, and exchange all these dreams for a little peace before he dies?

No, I will not be silent. My words shall avenge these unhappy creatures, broken under the dead weight of Russian absolutism, of this infernal régime which brings men to the brink of moral collapse, to a state of dream-like apathy.

We must speak out—otherwise no one will ever suspect how much that is both beautiful and sublime lies locked in the breasts of these brave men and will be buried with them when they die, under the snows of exile, in tombs that may not even bear their dishonoured names—their sacred names, rather, which their friends will preserve in their hearts but never dare breathe aloud.

We have only to open our mouths, only to murmur a few words about what we want or what we hope for, when at once they clamp down on us, and try to turn the cradle of free speech into its grave. How can we live like this?

At a certain moment the human intellect comes of age and when it does, it can no longer be kept in bondage, not in the chains of censorship nor in the leading-strings of prudence. When this happens, propaganda becomes one of nature's needs. For how can it be enough to whisper in our neighbour's ear, when even the knell of the tocsin may well fail to rouse him from his stupor?

From the revolt of the Streltsy[1] to the conspiracy of December the 14th, there was no serious political rising in Russia. The explanation is simple enough. Among the people at large there was no really coherent revolutionary movement. In some matters they found themselves in agreement with the Government, and on many others they took their opinions from the Government. Only the peasants, cut off from all the benefits of the Imperial régime and more oppressed than ever before, attempted a revolution. The whole of Russia from the Urals to Penza, Simbirsk and Kazan, was, for several months, under the sway of Pugachev. The Imperial army was forced to fall back before these Cossack onslaughts and General Bibikov who had been sent out from Petersburg to take over command, wrote back from Nijni Novgorod if I am not mistaken: 'Things are going very badly: the most frightening thing is not the armed hordes of the rebels, but the state of mind of the people which is bad, very bad.'

Finally, after the most incredible efforts, the insurrection was crushed. From that time onwards the people sank into a state of total apathy, dumbness, indifference.

But while the mass of the people slumbered the aristocracy showed signs of progress. Civilization slowly began to penetrate their consciousness, and, if we need real living proof of their political maturity, of their moral progress, which ultimately committed them to some form of action, we have those wonderful men, those heroes, of whom you have so well remarked that 'they, alone, in the very jaws of the dragon, attempted the bold blow of December the 14th.'

Their defeat and the terrorism of the present reign have succeeded in smothering all progressive ideas and putting a stop to any more of these premature attempts. Issues of a rather different sort have come to the fore: people are no longer prepared to risk their lives for a constitution, now

[1]The mutiny of the Streltsy regiments in 1698.

that they know that any Charter granted in Petersburg can always be neutralized by some chicanery on the part of the Tsar: the fate of the Polish constitution exists as a permanent warning.

For ten years, people struggled on at purely intellectual tasks, without ever risking a word, until eventually they found themselves in such a state of anxiety and depression that 'they threw away their lives for the pleasure of a moment's freedom', for the mere possibility of expressing something of what was in their minds.

Some, with that frivolity, that recklessness which is to be found only amongst Poles and Russians, gave up everything that they had and went abroad to try and find some distraction for their depression: others, unable to overcome the horror that they felt for the St Petersburg régime, buried themselves in the depths of their estates. The younger generation became immersed either in Panslavism or in German philosophy or in history or in economics: in a word, no one in Russia who felt any natural bent for intellectual matters either would or could remain idle and tranquil.

The recent case of Petrashevsky who was sentenced to the mines for life, and his friends who were deported in 1849, for organizing revolutionary clubs a stone's throw from the Winter Palace, adequately reveals, both in the bold recklessness of the victims, and in the obvious hopelessness of the undertaking, that the period of rational calculation is over, that the desire for action can no longer be thwarted, that people prefer running the certain risk of some punishment or other to remaining dumb, impassive witnesses of the Petersburg tyranny. There is a popular Russian fable that tells of a Tsar who, suspecting his wife of unfaithfulness, ordered her to be placed in a barrel with her son. The Tsar then had the barrel sealed and cast into the sea.

For many years the barrel floated on the waters. Meanwhile the young prince grew and grew, until he could touch the ends of the barrel with his head and his feet. Every day the lack of space proved more and more irksome to him. One day he said to his mother, 'O royal mother, allow me to stretch myself to my full length.'

'Tsarevitch, my son,' replied his mother, 'beware of doing what you say: for the barrel will burst and you will perish in the salt waves.' For a moment the Tsarevitch was silent, and then, having thought the matter over very carefully, he said: 'Royal mother, I will stretch myself. Better to stretch oneself in freedom once and then perish.'

There, Sir, you have our history.

It will be a black day for Russia when she can no longer find men who are willing to dare everything, whatever the risk, simply for the pleasure of stretching themselves in freedom once.

But there is no immediate danger of this. . . .

Involuntarily the name of Michael Bakunin comes before the mind. Bakunin has provided Europe with proof that a Russian can possess revolutionary ability.

I was deeply moved, Sir, by the noble words you used about him: unhappily these words will never reach him.

International crime has surpassed itself—Saxony handed the victim over to Austria: the Hapsburg despatched him to Nicholas. I am informed by friends in Petersburg that he is now in Russian hands. He is in Schlüsselburg, in that fortress of evil memory, once the prison of the young prince Ivan, the grandson of the Tsar Alexis, who was kept cooped up there like a wild animal, until he was murdered by Catherine the Second: she ordered his death herself, while her own hands were still stained with her husband's blood, and then had the wretched officer who had faithfully carried out her orders executed.

In that damp dungeon lapped by the icy waters of Lake Ladoga, Bakunin has already been tortured. The authorities know quite well that he will never speak—nor is there anything that they need to know from him—and yet they torture him[1]. . . . This is no place for dreams or hopes.

Let him then sleep his last sleep, let him die, for there is no way of rescuing him. A martyr betrayed by two treacherous Governments, each of which still holds in its bloody hands some morsels of his flesh. . . .

May his name be sacred, and avenged . . . but by whom? . . .

For all of us shall perish by the wayside; it will then fall to you, in your grave, sombre, majestic accents, to remind our children that they have a debt to discharge. . . .

I will conclude on this note, on the thought of this martyr. It is in his name and in mine that I warmly press your hand.

ALEXANDRE HERZEN

NICE MARITIME
September 1851

[1]'The author was misinformed. Bakunin remained, even now remains, in a casemate in Petersburg; and he was not tortured. Nicholas is reported to have said, after speaking with him: "He is a noble but dangerous madman. Such maniacs must not be permitted in the streets." '—Note to the translation of 1855.

In fact both Herzen and his original translator were misinformed. Bakunin was not tortured, he did not meet Nicholas, and he spoke. He sent the Tsar a 'confession' in which he professed to repent of his mutinous activities. This remarkable document was unknown and unpublished until after the revolution of 1917. Bakunin was sent to Siberia whence he escaped in 1859.